Mr. President, Say What?!

Dr. Thomas (Tom) Law

Mr. President, Say What?!
Copyright © 2018 by Thomas L. Law, III

Cover design by Bekah Law Production bekahlaw.com

Contact the author at: mr.presidentsaywhat@gmail.com

*Note to Kindle Unlimited Subscribers.

Leaf through the pages to the end of the book. Even if you do not read each page, the author receives a small amount for each page. If you want to help a struggling author, then leaf through all their books even if you do not read them. It will take you a few minutes, but the author will receive some compensation for their work.

Books by the author:

Mr. President, Say What?!

Wounded in Ministry: Finding Hope Through Forgiving

You Will Never Be the Same: Organizing a Group Trip to Israel or Enhancing Your Own Trip

The Church: One Man's Opinion
The Church: One Man's Opinion Numerical Growth
The Church: One Man's Opinion Spiritual Growth and Leadership
The Church: One Man's Opinion Ministry and Missions
The Church: One Man's Opinion Finances Place and Reproduction
The Church: One Man's Opinion Relationships
The Church: One Man's Opinion Connectedness

Developing a Baptist Association
Developing a Baptist Association Workbook
Developing a Baptist Association Teacher's Edition
La Asociación Bautista
La Asociación Bautista Libro de Trabajo
La Asociación Bautista Versión del Profesor

To my country...

CONTENTS

INTRODUCTION

Several years ago, I had a conversation with a friend who had grown up in a country ruled by a dictator. At the time, this friend worked for a non-profit. He was a man of enormous talent with ideas that would have transformed the non-profit where he worked. I asked him why he didn't speak up and share his ideas. He said, "the person who sticks up their head loses it." I looked at him quizzically and asked what he was talking about. He told me as he was growing up, he noticed that those who objected to what the dictator was doing often disappeared or were killed outright. He and most everyone else learned to keep their mouth shut and their head down. He said that it had become a way of life to survive.

Maybe I should have listened to my friend. After the last few months, I find it difficult to stay quiet. I hope that by highlighting the things I have seen, others will see what I see, and maybe a change will occur. I can't continue to keep my head down and be true to my values and my country. If I am going to be true to my country, I cannot continue to close my mouth and keep quiet. I need to speak up, hoping that someone will hear and do something about it.

As you read these musings, you will quickly realize that there are things and comments which triggered them. For anyone else, this might suggest that they are old hat, been there done that, and things have moved on. But with this President, things never move on. As you will see, the most insignificant event will thrust us back into a battle royal. Therefore, what may look out of date or passé is really as current as today's tweet and tomorrow's headline.

RESPECT

Honoring the office of President and, by extension, the person holding that office has been something that has been ingrained in me. Regardless of political persuasion, I have always understood that our responsibility is to honor and respect the President out of respect for our Country. This is not always easy especially depending on who is holding the office.

You, Mr. President, make this especially hard. Evidently, you grew up in a time and place which valued "throwing the first punch." In fact, it comes so naturally to you that you come across as a bully as you belligerently attack all of those who you feel are your opponents. By putting them down, you can climb on their backs and stand taller. That is what it would seem you are trying to do.

Unfortunately, I, too, grew up with aphorisms that mark me to this day. One of those is, "turnabout is fair play," which means in my mind that if I'm hit, I can hit back. Now physically hitting someone is not your weapon of choice, Mr. President. Yours are words and particularly caustic words and name-calling. Anyone you construe to be an opponent gets a moniker that is not very nice and sometimes downright mean. But no one better do it to you because you will hit back and hit back harder.

So, it would seem that you, Mr. President, also learned "turnabout is fair play." However, with the added caveat allowing the respondent to up the ante and, in their mind, get the last word. In other words, you not only hit back, but your goal is a knockout punch that will leave your opponent out of the race.

It is like watching the school yard bully in action. He never tires of ridiculing the other kid. The crowd rallies him on because they are not the ones being attacked. The crowd's cries animate him to go further and further regardless of how absurd and demeaning it gets.

Although he thinks he is demeaning the other person, the one being demeaned is himself. When this person is the President, it demeans him and the office itself, much to the detriment of all, including the Nation.

HATE-MONGERING

When you hear hateful words and fear tactics aimed at one ethnic group, it should alarm all of us. This has been the tactic of dictatorial leaders in the past. They have used these words to sway their base into giving up their basic moral decency and following these leaders down a dark path, one from which it is difficult to return.

Often it is unclear if the person spewing this nonsensical hatred believes what he or she is saying or is just using this as a ploy to sway their supporters. It is also unclear if those who support him believe what is being said or if they are just going along with the crowd. I'm afraid that too often, not only do those who form the lynch mob believe what is being spouted, but the leader is convinced as well.

This reflects the dark side of human nature, which thinks that it diminishes them if someone else has something. The concept comes from the mistaken notion that the pie is limited, and if someone else gets a piece, I will not get one. A corollary is that I am due a slice regardless of how inadequate and useless I am – it is my right. And if I am not given it, I will take it from those more deserving than me. This rhetoric then co-opts us into doing what we know we shouldn't and obtaining what is not rightfully ours.

And if the leader of the nation says it, then it must be right. Those Mexicans must be "bad people" because the President said they were. The Jews must be terrible because the Fuehrer (leader) said so. Regardless of what my experience is. Irrespective of how they have treated me. Regardless of what my eyes tell me, it must be so because those in leadership have said so.

My hope is that sanity will prevail amid this insanity. My dream is, that of Martin Luther King, Jr., that one day we will live in unity and the words of the United States Declaration of Independence will ring true – "We hold these truths to be self-evident, that all men are created equal, that they are endowed by their Creator with certain unalienable Rights, that among these are Life, Liberty, and the pursuit of Happiness."

INSECURITY AND NARCISSISM

This President is very insecure. In fact, I am not sure that we have ever had a President as insecure as this one. The way he lashes out at those who oppose him is a mark of his insecurity. He cannot stomach any contrary opinion. He doesn't want to know your view; he wants you to affirm him and his belief. There really is no use talking to him. He doesn't listen. He already has his mind made up.

But his insecurity plays itself out in other ways as well. One of which is his intense narcissism. This narcissism is so extreme that he is the best and most excellent at everything. Everything he does has to be the largest and most impressive thing ever done.

I began noticing this after the inauguration. I had not paid any attention to it before. However, I am sure that all the pre-election rallies were the largest and most spectacular ever held. The President could not stop talking about the "fact" that more people were present at his inauguration than ever before. What took me aback was not that he continued to hold this position in the face of visual proof but that he held it even after everyone else had moved on. It was as if everyone said this does not make any difference in the grand scheme of things. But obviously, to the President, it made a difference. If his inauguration attendance was not the largest, he was a failure.

Since then, it has only gotten worse. The latest is the President's assertion that he is so brave that, whereas trained police officers were reticent to run into a building where an active shooter was killing seventeen people, he would have run in even if he did not have a gun with which to defend himself. In his mind, he is so all-powerful that he would have attacked and subdued the gunman with his own hands. I believe that this is the classic definition of hubris.

I laughed the other day when the President was televised talking about the bald spot on the back of his head. Frankly, I have not seen the bald spot, and when it was reported that the President has a prescription for a lotion to prevent male baldness, I thought it very strange. He has a massive head of hair, of which he is, justifiably, very proud. I think someone has played a nasty trick on the President. They have told him that he is getting bald in a place where it is challenging, if not impossible, for him to see. Because he is so vain, he believed them and has begun taking action to overcome this issue. I would guess those who set him up are laughing their heads off.

THE ELECTION

It would seem that the 2016 election will never go away. The President, time and again, comes back to it like a bad nightmare. It so galls him that he did not win the popular vote that he cannot move on past that event. Something must be wrong with the reporting. Obviously, the news media was in collusion with his opponents. There must have been a mistake in the counting of the ballots. Or something else must have happened. Because there is no way that he, the greatest, most admired person, with the largest following in history, would not have gotten the most votes.

In those moments when he seems like he has accepted the election results, he points out, although with some difficulty, that it is much harder to gain a majority of the Electoral College vote than it is to achieve a majority of the popular vote. Obviously, this is a ploy to put him on top once again, but how could it be that anyone in their right mind would have voted against him, much less that his opponent got more votes than he did.

The other thing the President seems to put forward from time to time is that there must have been millions of fraudulent votes casts. The obvious culprit in the President's mind is the millions of undocumented illegal aliens who live in the United States. Given his opposition to them staying, they must have signed up in record numbers to vote for his opponent. In collusion with the election officials, they then padded the ballots, creating a disparity between him and his opponent.

Despite the protest by most election officials around the country, this could not have occurred. The President remains convinced that the voter's fraudulent registration caused the popular vote to indicate that he did not win the majority vote. The majority will of the popular vote was taken from him by those who are in this country illegally.

In his view, the majority of Americans would vote only for him. Therefore, the only explanation is that the popular majority was stolen from him. It is these fraudulently registered voters that caused this aberration to take place. Otherwise, the record would reflect the reality of his supremacy, not only in the Electoral College but also in the popular vote count.

WHO WON THE 2016 ELECTION?

Almost two years since the election took place, that question seems totally out of place unless you listen to the President. As mentioned above, early on, he questioned the vote. There does not seem to be anything about the election that is not up for grabs and in doubt.

Did agents of the government try to undermine his campaign? Did people infiltrate his organization to gather incriminating evidence to use against him? Did elements opposing his candidacy colluded to make it impossible for him to win? These and other questions seem to be at the forefront of the President's agenda. One would think, from reading these headlines and tweets, the President lost the election and was trying to determine what nefarious elements cause him to lose.

This, of course, brings me back to my original question. Did you win the election, Mr. President, or do you know something the rest of us do not? Did someone else win, and you are trying to determine how they stole the election from you? Your rhetoric would suggest that this is the case. Your tweets would indicate that someone kept you from your stated goal of becoming President. Your demands for investigations and attempt to uncover these miscreants make us think that we have all been duped by you, and you really are not the President.

If you are, in fact, the President, then those who were spying on you to undermine your campaign did not do a good job. They must have been lousy and should have been fired. Since many (maybe not all) of your machinations were on the front page of every paper and filled every newsfeed, they would not have had to do much to find something with which to fill many dossiers, not just one.

Obviously, all this hoopla which you are raising has nothing to do with some hidden double agent trying to find dirt on you. That was too easy to find without using nefarious means. Mr. President, you must be trying to distract the American public and those investigating you. You must be trying to absorb all our time looking for ghosts so that we will not have any energy, money, or time to find out what really was going on.

This is the only realistic explanation. You are blowing smoke everywhere, not just up our skirts, so we will not see what really happened and get to the bottom of what must be a tragic miscarriage of justice. Whatever it is must be so monumental and transformative that you are doing everything you can to make sure we do not find it. But the bigger stink you make and the more you holler, the more apparent there is something there if we will just keep looking.

COAL

The President's hype about beautiful clean coal reminds me of other misguided promises and decisions made in the past. I know he is playing to his base and trying to garner votes, but surely, he is more intelligent than those comments would allow. Transitions are complicated, and adjusting to new paradigms requires real leadership rather than trite hyperbole.

It reminds me of a couple of other paradigm shifts that have left workers wondering where their future is. About a hundred years ago, the world was moving away from the horse and buggy and had begun embracing a future with a horseless carriage (car). Companies who continued holding onto the past, trying as hard as possible to make a better buggy, were left in the dust. The companies who transitioned from making buggies to thinking of themselves as "carriage" designers, like Cadillac, began creating a future for themselves. They embraced their past and used it as a springboard for the future. They even immortalized it in the carriage logo, which each new car carried as it made its way down the assembly line.

We find the same scenario some fifty years later in Switzerland.
In 1968, Switzerland had 65% of the world market share [of the watch industry] and according to expert estimations, more than 80% of the profits. Yet, just ten

years later, their market share had fallen below 10%, and in the ensuing three years, they had to release 50,000 of their 65,000 watch workers. Today, Japan dominates the world of watchmaking. In 1968, Japan had virtually no market share. The Swiss watch industry was put back to zero by a paradigm shift. The Quartz Movement watch: Totally electronic. A thousand times more accurate than the mechanical watches it replaced. Battery-powered. All-new rules.

The Swiss themselves invented this revolutionary design at their research laboratories in Neuchâtel. Yet, when their own researchers presented this idea to the Swiss watch manufacturers in 1968, they rejected it. After all, it didn't have any bearings. It didn't require a lot of gears. It didn't even have a mainspring. It had none of the marvelous mechanical complexity the Swiss were so good at. Therefore, it couldn't possibly be the future of watches.

So confident were the Swiss manufacturers in that conclusion that they didn't even protect the idea. Later that year, the researchers displayed that watch for all to see at the World Watch Congress. Seiko of Japan walked past, took one look, and the rest is history." Pages 13-14, Classic Consolidation 1.4, 8/2/01, Copyright 2001, Joel A. Barker.

Coal still has its uses, and some may find it beautiful, but I don't know anyone, except the President, who would call it clean. The world is moving on. Unless we move on, we will suffer the same disastrous results which overwhelmed the buggy and Swiss watch industries. Others will not only take our jobs but our future as well.

RUSSIA

There is no doubt that the Russian's meddled in the American political scene. This has been going on for decades, I am sure. Ever since the Russians came on the world scene and moved beyond focusing on their part of Europe and Asia. But they are not the only ones. Every country with any reach meddles in the internal affairs of those countries with whom they have contact, particularly if they feel threatened by those countries.

The United States has been involved in the internal politics of every country with whom we have ever related. Sometimes overtly and sometimes covertly. We have set up zones of influence (Monroe Doctrine, among others) where we have told other world powers to stay out; this is our territory and to leave it alone. Over the years, world powers have challenged us. Even those within the zones of influence have rebelled against the United States' sovereignty. This is nothing new and should not come as a surprise.

An example of how other countries have meddled in our elections and may have even changed the election is the United States' relationship with Iran. When the Shah was overthrown, the United States was painted as evil because it had been involved in maintaining the Shah's dictatorship for many years. The United

States Embassy was sacked, and the State Department employees were taken prisoner.

The United States tried through various means – diplomatic and military – to achieve their release. Most of those attempts failed, and President Carter took it on the chin. His political future was in jeopardy. His only hope was negotiating the release of the hostages so that he could regain the support of the American people. The leadership of Iran was well aware of this and dragged their feet. The hostages were released once the new President (Reagan) took office. He got all the credit and his predecessor all the blame. If that isn't meddling, I don't know what is.

Of course, in the mind of President Trump, there was no collusion. He is a businessman. You make contacts with people, work with people, even those with whom you disagree. You develop projects together and even work toward the same objectives. This is not collusion; this is just good business sense. If they can help you achieve your goals, you use them as long as it is to your benefit, and then you kick them to the curb.

I am confident that it has never ever entered the President's mind that the President of Russia (Putin), much less anyone of lesser stature, could use him. He does that to others, but no one has ever done that to him. His ego would not allow him to think that, much less permit others to accuse him of being that naïve. Therefore, everyone else is lesser and subject to manipulation, but not him. He is above being controlled and would know it if anyone were to try. How do you collude with someone inferior to you? Colluding would elevate that person or organization to your level. You use inferior people; you do not collude with them.

What's more, President Trump admires how the Russian President takes charge and deals with those who oppose him. That is what a strong leader does. A strong leader does not abide by those who oppose him. A strong leader puts them in their place and makes sure that they no longer are a bother. That's leadership, and President Trump admires that style of leadership.

These same characteristics are found in Kim Jon Un, but the President does not hold him in the same regard as the Russian President. It would seem that there is a simple reason for this fact. North Korea is small and fragile and can really only jab at the United States. Their President's ability to hurt this Country is minimal. Therefore, he is not someone whom the United States President would regard with much esteem.

It's interesting how much the Russian and North Korean Presidents have in common with President Trump. While both countries need help becoming "great again," President Trump thinks the United States does. Therefore, all three are doing what they believe will make their countries great. Unfortunately, this means putting the rest of the world at risk.

PROFANITY

To his credit, the President does not often use profanity or obscenities in his speeches or on Twitter. Sometimes, though, he does fall into this habit when speaking off-the-cuff or thinks he is behind closed doors. There are two ways of seeing this. He thinks this is a way to connect with his audience, with his base. Or, two, his education and intellect are so limited that he finds it hard to construct a meaningful sentence in any way other than falling back on the tried and true locker-room language.

Unfortunately, it often comes across as demeaning. The President actually seems to be dumbing down his rhetoric to reach those he thinks are beneath him. After all, he did go to the best schools. And is sharper than almost anyone. Therefore, he needs to say things the average Joe will understand. Because if he were to speak like he usually does, then his base would not understand him or vote for him.

This comes across as demeaning, condescending, and disparaging. But most of all, it comes across as condescending. Those people who voted for him and now support him without question really cannot understand him. They are unquestioningly (some would say unthinkingly) loyal to him. He even bragged about this when he proclaimed, he would not lose any of his followers' even if he were to stand in the middle of the street and shoot someone. They blindly follow him. He knows it and uses it to his advantage.

Profanity and obscenities are a sign of a weak mind. Anyone who uses them is taking the easy way out. There are so many more insightful and colorful ways of saying things about others than to resort to the use of obscenities reveals the limited vocabulary the speaker possesses. Not only does it speak to his limited lexicon, but it also shows his lack of creativity and small-mindedness.

You would think the "best" schools gave the President a better education. I would hope that his background would have prepared him better, and he would be able to communicate important information in some way other than the use of simple profanities.

This then leads me to the conclusion that he, in fact, is demeaning his base by speaking down to them. At some time, this will come back to create problems for him and his presidency. Not one likes for someone else to think that they are superior. As his base sees this "talk" for what it is – condescension and disdain – they will begin to turn on him, and he will reap what he has sown.

THE TRUTH

The truth is a variable and hard-to-pin-down reality when it comes to the President. In his estimation, if he has said it, it is true. If it agrees with what he has said, it is the truth. If it in any way contradicts him or his positions, there is no way that it can be anything close to the truth.

Therefore, what others see as him telling lies is just his understanding of what is going on. He is not telling lies. He never lies or cheats (even at golf). There is a narrative that he carries through life. If something is said that goes against this narrative, this must be a lie. That is why he calls much of what comes from the media FAKE NEWS. It goes against his narrative and, therefore, must not be accurate. He downplays other media outlets in favor of Fox News because the latter affirms his narrative and supports his perspective.

He also eschews the government's intelligence community because much of what they share with him is contrary to his beliefs. He is a product of his background and his upbringing. As he grew up, television was the most trusted source for information. He continues to look to this medium for insight into what is going on around him, even though he has at his command one of the most extraordinary intelligence operations in the world.

But this source of information comes from government employees and is, therefore, suspect. It is biased, and the more that it contradicts his own narrative, the more erroneous it must be. He is the ultimate arbiter of truth, and whatever goes against what he believes is false.

He can't depend even on those people he has named to specific roles because now they have become government employees. Therefore, he must maintain his one means of communicating with the American public – Twitter. This forum allows him to circumvent the media and present his narrative and perspective on the facts. It also allows him to do an end-run around his own staff, giving him direct access to those people who remain loyal to him.

LIAR

"Liar, liar pants on fire". The juvenile school yard taunt comes to mind when thinking about the President. I have no doubt that he has heard it before and even been taunted by it. His propensity to lie did not just begin when he started running for office. This pattern must have started when he was in grade school or before. Somehow, he perceived rewards for having done it, and it has become easier as the years have gone by.

At this point, it is a bragging event. How he goes into a meeting and talks about things of which he has no knowledge. He makes it up as he goes along. He tells one whopper after another. And he even doubles down when confronted by actual facts which refute his lies.

Even when wrong, for him, there is no backing down. He has to be right even when he knows that he is making it up and there is video or audio evidence to refute him. But since he said it, it must be accurate, and those who defy him are wrong. If it supports his narrative, it must be fact. Since his report is correct and he thinks he is on a "holy" mission, whatever he utters will be found out to be the most trustworthy of statements.

His backers, I am sure, often groan and say, "There he goes again." His opponents call him on it, but to no avail. Our nation's allies who are caught in the middle of his belligerence don't know what to do. They want to trust us, but how can they when the President constantly prefabricates to support his narrative. Those with whom we are closest as a nation don't know if we will have their back or not. Those who oppose us are laughing.

EVANGELICALS

Often those who claim to be evangelicals are called hypocrites. The taunt comes as they are perceived to say one thing and yet practice another. The mantra those who have problems with the evangelicals perceive is "do as I say, not as I do." Of course, no one respects someone who seems to be two-faced, whose life does not live what they preach.

This has never seemed more accurate than now as they coalesce around the President. Here is a person who is a self-proclaimed womanizer (remember the interview with Billy Bush) and voyeur (remember him bragging about seeing women backstage half-dressed at the Miss Universe Pageant), and yet evangelicals still support him. Here is a person who consistently lies and brags about his abuse of people (You're Fired!), and yet evangelicals call for unity behind "their" man.

An evangelical pastor sluffs it off, stating we are all sinners. The President should not be held to a higher standard than anyone else. This may be true, but should we go to the lowest basest level. Shouldn't we hold anyone who aspires to give leadership to the country to a higher standard? Shouldn't we expect more from those who wish to represent us?

While we are talking about standards, don't the evangelical churches expect a higher standard from those who lead them? Don't they presume that their pastors hold to a higher moral lifestyle? Don't these pastors, in turn, owe it to their communities to speak truth not only from the pulpit but also in their everyday life? Shouldn't these church leaders be the first to call a sin a sin instead of just pushing it under the rug claiming that it's the "fallen" world in which we live?

Maybe the term hypocrite is not unwarranted in this situation. Perhaps these leaders are speaking out of both sides of their mouths. If so, is it any wonder that the youth of America is calling into question whether they can believe anything these leaders say.

WEALTH

Money is very important to the President although he makes a big deal of the fact that he and others, his son-in-law, for instance, do not take a salary. My guess is that the salary is small potatoes compared to the significant income generated for his brand by his actions. An example of this is his perennial use of his own properties for government events. I'm sure each of these properties charges top dollar to the government for their use, and the President's bottom line is benefited.

There seems to be a smoke and mirrors quality to all the talk about money. Maybe that is why he is so reticent to disclose his tax returns. He may, and probably doesn't, have nearly as much as he claims. This goes back to his narrative. In his mind, he is one of, if not the wealthiest person in the world. This, regardless of facts presented by others. Those who offer these facts just are not aware of the vast amount of wealth which he has, nor will they ever know precisely what he has. He thinks he is wealthy, and, therefore, he is.

The illusionary aspect of this comes into play when you realize that he is a master at using other people's resources to make himself look good. At present, he uses the total resources of the United States government. He has hundreds of thousands of people at his beck and call. He can do anything he wants, and no one can hold him accountable since the President is immune to questioning. This plays into his narrative and enhances his own perspective of himself.

Therefore, in his opinion, whatever bottom line his detractors discover is not reality. Since what he has is his and what you have is his, there is no end to what he has available to him. What's more, once it has served his purpose to get him where he wants to be, he puts it aside and moves on to the next shill he needs for his self-aggrandizement.

Currently, his shill is the conservative right from flyover America. He found a message that resonated with them, and the more he repeated it, the more they gravitated to him. But he does not believe what he is spouting. He is just using them to further his own persona. Other than enhancing himself, he really does not have a plan. Once this particular group has served its purpose, he will put them aside and begin looking for the next foil. And on and on, it will go until someone finally is tired of the bait and switch.

LOYALTY

Loyalty in the President's mind seems to be a one-way street. It means being loyal to him, but he does not feel that same compulsion toward anyone else. In fact, he seems to use people and throw them away when he is finished getting out of them what he needs.

On the other hand, he demands unfettered loyalty to himself. Anyone whom he does not see as loyal to him personally is doomed. It is not enough to be devoted to the nation or to the position; he demands utter and total abject personal loyalty or your out. Any hint that there is any disloyalty on your part and you're doomed.

This perceived disloyalty may not be seen by anyone else. In fact, others may think that you have "sold out." But if the President believes you have been disloyal in any way, then it is a done deal; you are out.

Often we think of disloyalty as something that is done or said. In the President's case, he has widened the margins by which he judges the loyalty of those around him. This new wider margin includes things that are said and done, but something he perceives should not have been done. Even those things ethics and legal standards demand but which he feels are counterproductive to what he would like to accomplish are disloyalty.

That is to say, he is the supreme judge of loyalty. He is also the ultimate decision-maker for what should and shouldn't be done. He can't abide by independent thinkers or actors. Everything has to be under his control, and if it is not, then something is very wrong.

YOU'RE FIRED

The Attorney General finally did his master's bidding. The President had been badgering him for months. Badmouthing him and ridiculing him personally and professionally. Now he has saved his job, at least for the next few days.

The President has no regard for anyone other than himself. Anything that he perceives as contrary to him he opposes. It's not just that he opposes that person; he must crush him or her in the process. He believes that the only way he can stand out is on the shoulders (you might say heads) of those he has conquered. The image of him as the conqueror with his foot on his enemy's head is very apt.

The President had hoped to accomplish two things. One was to cast a shadow on the FBI, the Special Prosecutor, and the investigation. The other was to punish someone whom he deemed had betrayed him. Along the way, it would not be too much a stretch to see him demeaning an underling by forcing him to do something which fundamentally went against his personal ethical standards. For the President, this is part of the fun. If he can get someone else to violate their own ethics, it makes him feel better because of his own lack of ethical standards. Those who have values bother him. He would rather everyone be as lacking as he is. In fact, he thinks they are, and part of his role is to bring out that hypocrisy in their lives. They put on a façade which he believes is a lie.

Unfortunately for him, he does not understand how Washington works. Whereas the former second in command of the FBI, Andrew McCabe, would have faded into the woodwork as he retired now, he has become a significant figure. Others are coming to his aid, and there is no doubt that he will not only gain his pension, but he will also be able to write a book, and he will be able to go on a talking circuit should he so desire. In other words, while the President had the intent to punish him, he now will come out of this wealthier and more important than ever. It is another example of the President doing something without understanding the unintended consequences of his actions.

TWITTER

Really, Mr. President. Is that any way to treat someone who has served you, and especially the country, well? I understand your desire to have someone with whom you can work. Your need to have someone who sees eye to eye with you is understandable as well. Although you have stated that you enjoy and want people around you who have different perspectives than your own, your actions belie that position. Of course, that is your prerogative. You can name anyone you wish to your cabinet.

I applauded your desire to have those around you who come to the table with different understandings of the events which currently beset the country. I thought that it spoke highly of you that you were willing to hear other points of view and that you would be informed by those differences. Before the election, your actions and comments did not give a lot of credibility to your words, but I was willing to take you at your word until proven otherwise.

Your actions since the elections and now your statements clarifying that you are finally putting together the cabinet you need tell a different story. You need to be surrounded by people who agree with you. But more importantly, you need to be surrounded by people who will knuckle under to your will. You cannot stomach someone who speaks his or her own mind. Your perspective is the only one that counts, and your understanding of reality is the only truth you need. Those who differ need not apply.

Be that as it may, and you certainly do have the right to have those people you want on your team, the way you treat people makes me wonder why anyone would want to associate with you, much less be on your team. Simple courtesies would call for you to speak to people personally should you disagree with them instead of publicly calling them out and ridiculing them. Picking up the phone or, better yet, inviting them into your office, after all, they are at your beck and call, would be more appropriate than sending out a tweet which they receive at the same time (or in some cases after) the general public hears about it. That is just not how to treat people regardless of who you are, especially if you are the United States of America President.

As if that were not enough, you then turn around and call someone who was ushered out of the White House because they could not get a security clearance due to financial or moral issues. And to add insult to injury, you tell him he has gotten a rotten deal and hire him to your reelection campaign. What kind of message are you trying to send us?

BOASTING

One of the most notable characteristics of the President is his propensity to boast. He boasts about anything and everything as long as he thinks it makes him look good. Boasting has one purpose: to draw attention to his greatness and how indispensable he is.

It is interesting how readily he takes credit for things over which he has no control and is silent about things that are well within his arena of influence. Take the Stock Market. Whenever it goes up, regardless of the reason, the first to take credit for its rise is the President. The further it rises, the more it, obviously, is due to his overwhelming greatness.

At the same time, should the Stock Market go down, he is silent. I was tempted to say strangely mute, but there is nothing strange about his silence. Anything that is negative or would cast a negative light on him cannot be his fault. He only produces positive results. If he cannot explain something or something looks like it might shine a negative light on him, it baffles him and leaves him speechless.

He has no words for something which cannot really be happening. He is running the country better than anyone who has ever occupied the White House. Obviously, he has done nothing wrong. Therefore, those who have chosen to undermine his greatness by orchestrating the fall of the Stock Market indexes must be out to get him, and it baffles him. How dare they? What audacity leads them to believe that they can do anything that hurts him?

He is going to succeed. You can bet your future on that. And even when he might fail at something (like needing to take a company – maybe even the country – into bankruptcy), it is only allowing him to gear down in order to move ahead of the competition.

He is a sure thing and if you don't believe it, just ask him.

MAKE AMERICA GREAT AGAIN

There are several problems with this slogan. One, it presumes that America does not continue to be great. In other words, it presumes that at some point, America stopped being a great country, and it is going to take someone like the President to help it achieve greatness once again.

For the vast majority of the country, America has always been great, and there is nowhere else on Earth they would rather live. They are proud to be Americans and think that this is the greatest country anywhere. Therefore, for this group, this slogan does not ring true.

There is another group of people for whom America has never been great. They are mostly those left out of the advances in the standard of living. These are the disenfranchised, those who have never been able to get to that next rung on the ladder. Those who have been left out and, often, pushed down. America has never been great for these people, so the "again" part of the slogan does not ring true to them. They have no understanding of what that may mean.

It would seem that the President is speaking to a small segment of American society who has fallen down a rung or two on the socioeconomic ladder. These are people who have lost their job and have not gotten a new one. Some of these can't get another job because they are not equipped to do anything other than what they had done. Others find themselves in a situation where the companies for whom they worked have changed, and they have not been able or willing to change with those companies. For still others, life circumstances have created situations that have caused them to move to a lower standard of living. Whatever the cause, it would seem that many of these people are angry about their circumstances.

The problem for this last group is there is no one solution to fix all the issues they present. It depends on where they live, the industry in which they were involved, and the issues that created these problems. The slogan then becomes a trite platitude used to manipulate these people rather than help them.

It would seem what is being said is what is good for the President is good for America and vice versa. They are one and the same. There is no difference between America and the President. What's more, he is the final arbiter of what it means to Make America Great. And the deciding factor is whether it helps him get elected and stay in power.

Since the issues are complex and challenging to solve, a solution will not be forthcoming. In fact, it would seem that the President really does not know how to solve them. And that shouldn't surprise anyone because no one else does either. Unfortunately, those who are pinning their hopes on him to wave a magic wand and cure these ills will be disappointed and probably eventually turn on him for disappointing them. Of course, suppose he can continue to throw them crumbs of hope along the way. In that case, he may be able to serve one or even two terms before they come to understand that he was never going to help them overcome the issues that are causing America not to be great for them.

KEEP AMERICA GREAT

It is interesting that the President has made his new campaign slogan – Keep America Great. After one year in office, he has cured all the ills which he railed against, and now America is a great country once again. His new role is to maintain the greatness he has achieved.

How naïve and egotistical can one man be? Not only has he not cured any of the ills which beset the country, everything that has happened during his first year in office can be considered a carryover from his predecessor. It takes time to begin implementing change, and a year will not do it. Therefore, whatever bragging rights are in the offing at this time belong to someone else, not the person currently in office.

Maybe things are moving in the right direction, but I am not feeling it. Even the oft-cited tax cut is in trouble. Interestingly enough, it is the same kind of trouble he railed against in the predecessor's significant initiative. These two huge bills have problems that only become apparent as they are implemented. This demonstrates how complex modern life is and especially current political life. It also shows how important it is to work together to make things better instead of just complaining about what is wrong.

Unfortunately, since his party was not willing to work to bring about a better product for his predecessor, the opposition is not inclined to help him improve his product. So rather than a new and improved America, we will continue with the broken one we had before – at least broken politically. As mentioned elsewhere, America continues to be a great country. The envy of the world. The place thousands would like to come to improve their lives and the lives of their children. But our political system is broken, divisive, and partisan. There is no desire to cooperate to help make the final product better. Partisan politicians are only interested in finger-pointing and climbing over those they oppose to get ahead. Mind you, not to move the country forward, but to get ahead personally and politically. Can anything be sadder?

The President sets the course for this trajectory. His name-calling and ridiculing of those he perceives as his enemies makes it easy for others to follow his example. Those who would be like him use vitriolic language to paint their opponents with harsh criticism, often untrue and unfounded. As the President has proven, it does not make any difference. Saying it tarnishes others and allows him to move ahead atop the charred remains of those he perceived stood in his way.

If he can do it, why not make that the standard for all? Why not craft your course using these same scorch earth tactics regardless of the consequences? After all, it got the President to where he is, and it will get me where I want to be. It doesn't matter if the whole country is burned to a crisp in the process.

THE WALL

We already have a wall on the border, and it does not seem to be working. Large sections of the border with Mexico either have a wall or some natural barrier, making it difficult to cross. An iconic picture that made the rounds some time back shows a group of innovative Mexicans with a jack they had strategically placed under one of the wall's panels. They would jack the panel high enough for someone to crawl under and lower it when the last person had crossed the border. The jack was then buried, ready for the next time it was needed.

Those determined to smuggle drugs and other illicit goods across the border find their own way. They dig tunnels to move their wares or use drones to ferry the merchandise over the wall. Innovative and creative people will always find ways to circumvent whatever barriers are created.

Hadrian's Wall, The Great Wall of China, The Berlin Wall, and the wall around my house robbers climbed three times to steal, all proved futile. Even walls with security guards like the one around the White House seem porous at times. If a person is determined to get through, there is not much we can do.

It would seem that to a large extent, walls only prove to be a deterrent to the kind of people who would be an asset, not to those who are bent on causing problems. Look at the wall in Bagdad, which surrounds the "Green Zone." It has not stopped bombers determined to create havoc. Or look at the formidable wall which the Israeli's have built to "protect" themselves from the Palestinians. Those who want to undermine Israeli security seem to find a way.

In fact, history tells us that walls don't work because they don't address the underlying issue. And, most often, the underlying problem is a disparity between those on each side of the wall. Rather than spending 20 billion (and I don't know anyone except maybe you, Mr. President, who thinks it will be built for that amount) on a wall, why don't we use the money to change the socioeconomic divide that created the need for a wall in the first place? Of course, that would mean making the world a great place to live rather than just focusing on making America like some illusionary memory of what it may have been.

THE WALL 2.0

It was bound to happen. What is surprising is that it took so long. Finally, the President "wizened up." Yes, I'm aware that the word does not mean wiser like it sounds. It means wrinkled, lined, creased, shriveled (up), withered, weather-beaten, shrunken, gnarled, and aged. But that is precisely what must have happened because the last word I would use to describe the President is "wise." He is many things, but he is not that. But as they say, even a broken clock is right twice a day.

I thought for sure that the President would have made a trip to the border with Mexico within the first month, especially to the construction site where a wall is being built between the two countries. While there on that photo op, I thought for sure he would have boasted about the campaign promise he was keeping by constructing the wall. Given how easily lies flow from his mouth and how loose he is with the truth, I fully expected that he would show the American public how diligent he had been about building what everyone seemed to want. "A big beautiful wall" (although no one calls what is there beautiful). But it did not happen quite that way. Yes, he went to the border but didn't congratulate himself, at that time, for the construction of the wall. I was shocked.

Now it has happened over a year into his presidency. He has told the world and especially his followers, that he has finally made good on building the wall. Although the money used was already in the pipeline long before he became President. And although it really is an extension of the same wall he mocked while running for office, he now is taking credit for it.

Finally, maybe we can now get off the subject and move on to some more significant issues. Maybe now that we have a wall, we can begin to address the real problem, which is the bizarre conglomeration of immigration laws that beset those wishing to legalize their status in the United States. Maybe now we can focus on building better relationships with our neighbors rather than criticizing and deriding them. Perhaps now we can become the country the world has admired for decades rather than the bully we have become in the last few months.

LEGISLATION

The President has no clue how the government works, and Congress has no idea how to work with a clueless President. He thinks that all he needs to do is say something, and it is law. After all, that is how it works in his companies. If it doesn't get done the way he wants it done, the person or persons are fired.

Like his predecessors, he has become enamored with Executive Actions because of the dysfunctionality of Congress. But even in these, neither he nor his staff understands how they work. This is one reason these actions have been mired down in the court system so often.

The House leadership has told him that they will not present new legislation unless they are convinced, he will sign it. His party controls both houses, making it easy for him to get something he wants to be passed. But, unfortunately, they are waiting for him to present them with a concrete, viable proposal, and he is waiting for them to send him something to sign.

It looks like we will continue to be stuck in the same quagmire, which bogged down his predecessors who did not control both houses as he does. He, though, does not know how to get things moving except to yell, harangue, and ridicule, in very vague and often conflicting ways, those around him for not doing what he has said.

Well, at least, there won't be a lot for his successor to clean up since he will not have accomplished anything.

IMMIGRATION

It is interesting that one of the reasons given for the Declaration of Independence was the mishandling of immigration on the part of the British Sovereign. How ironic that over two hundred years later, our present government is still dealing with this issue and, if I may say so, dealing with it as poorly as it was handled when all of this began.

People are making their way into our country. The vast majority of those people come seeking a better life for themselves and their families. Yes, some likely immigrate to the United States to cause us harm, but that has been going on for a long time. Maybe ever since this all began. Some even are successful in their attempts, but their number is minimal.

We are in the process of creating rules based on a reactionary response to a perceived ill. These are not constructive, nor do they reflect the changing world in which we live. To a large degree, they are attempting to win the war just waged. They are closing the barn door after the horses have run away.

People may use the immigration process to gain entry into the country wanting to do bad things, but if they can't immigrate here, they will find another way. Therefore, our immigration laws need to be proactive.

It is my experience that most of those here illegally would love to gain legal status. These illegals are hardworking, bright people who have undergone significant trials to live in this country. Even while living here, they continue to be abused by those wanting to take advantage of their illegal status to use them for their own ends. They are willing to submit to this kind of abuse because it is so much better than where they are from.

In most cases, they do the jobs which no one else wants to do. Like the Chinese were imported in the 19th century to build our railroad, this new wave of immigrants is here filling roles that otherwise would have to be exported to other parts of the world because no one in the United States wants to do them. Then where would the management and auxiliary jobs be that support these industries?

They understand that there is no pathway to citizenship, and they will never be able to take advantage of the Social Security taxes they pay each month. They don't care because they live better, and their children have the possibility of a future. There is no path to citizenship because our immigration laws are broken, and Congress is unwilling to do what is necessary to fix them. But those in the country illegally are willing to stay and suffer.

IMMIGRANTS

If a person makes it thousands of miles across hostile territories and through difficult, sometimes perilous, conditions, this may be the very person we need to help our country move forward. The United States is a land of immigrants. No one in the country is a decedent from someone who did not immigrate to this land. It is generally agreed even those referred to as Native Americans came from Asia, although long before the rest of us. All our ancestors had the drive and gumption to move from where they were to seek a better life for themselves and their progeny.

Over the last few centuries, it has been this new blood that had propelled the country forward. Those who come behind are driven to attain something better than they had. They, in turn, drive those who are here to do better as well. As business knows, competition is good. In fact, we have laws against monopolies to foster just this aspect of human nature.

It is my contention that those who are striving to arrive now are just as driven as our forefathers were. These young men and women want something better. They are escaping difficult situations where they were born. Instead of giving in to the status quo or joining the baser instincts of those around them, they seek new places where they can thrive. As they succeed, then they help the country thrive.

Anyone who is willing to travel thousands of miles under challenging circumstances and against great odds shows a determination that few others have. Those who make the effort to move out of the "comforts" of the known and are willing to risk the unknown show a trait that is needed and often in short supply. They show that barriers and obstacles will not hold them back. They demonstrate a "can do" attitude which propels them and their families forward. They help others see what can be rather than settling for what is. Isn't that the country we want? Aren't those the kinds of people who made America great? Aren't those the types of people who will make America great again?

NEW RULES

The rules and regulations – especially those made after 9/11 – reflect old thinking. They not only are reactionary, but those making these rules do not understand that the world changed between flights three and four on that fateful day. Until flight 3 (American Airlines Flight 77), it was a general understanding that those who highjacked airplanes wanted to live. The response to highjacking was to give the highjacker whatever they wanted with the understanding that if that happened, everyone would go home. But by flight 4 (United Airlines Flight 93), it became clear that we no longer lived in that world. These highjackers were making a statement and had decided not to live. It was up to those on the plane to try something different if they wanted to live. Since then, several high-jackings have been thwarted by passengers on the plane. They know the rules have changed even if the government does not.

The government created the TSA (Transportation Security Administration) because they do not recognize this new world in which we live. They are still trying to govern the old one even as everyone else is moving into the new one. But unfortunately, the rules (and world) have changed in many ways, and the government continues to play catch-up, although not very successfully.

The rules of school security changed on April 20, 1999, at Columbine High School. On September 15, 1999, at Wedgwood Baptist Church (Fort Worth, Texas), they changed for other public places like churches. And yet, almost twenty years later, we are still trying to respond as if we live in a world that has not changed. We teach students, teachers, and the general public to run, hide, and play dead while gunmen patrol the halls of our public places, killing at will. We look to training for police officers, soldiers and now arming teachers to solve the problem.

Like those on United Airlines Flight 93, it is really up to those who want to live to respond. Instead of running, hiding, or playing dead, why don't we teach our youth and the general public to fight back? The simple act of throwing things – after all, everyone has a phone they can throw – will distract the shooter long enough for others to tackle him. But it also will throw his aim off, and the bullets may hit the ceiling instead of a person. Anything is better than just waiting like sheep to be shot.

SHOOTINGS

Mass shootings, particularly those in schools, have created a public relations nightmare for the administration. The main reason is that they do not coincide with the narrative the administration is trying to create. In their minds, the only people who would do such an atrocious thing are those who want to undermine the very fabric of our country. Those would-be terrorists, illegals, and other unsavory characters who have invaded our country to create chaos.

The fact that most of those who have participated in these events have been native-born seems to be beside the point. I have thought that one morning I might wake up to the following NEWS ALERT!

LATE BREAKING NEWS FROM THE WHITE HOUSE

Washington, DC February 24, 2018 – We have just received a copy of a document the White House staff is preparing for the President to sign. It is an Executive Order requiring all schools in the United States to become hardened against the onslaught of young mentally impaired teenagers flooding America's streets. The President will order all military personnel to be deployed to encircle every school until such time as the Department of Homeland Security can create the School Security Administration (SSA). The SSA will take over securing American schools once it is fully functional. Until such time the United States military is charged with this role. To mitigate the court implementation of the Posse Comitatus Act, *the President will institute Marshal Law until the SSA is up and running.*

The Army Corp of Engineers will be instructed to harden school sites following these guidelines. An impenetrable wall at least thirty feet tall will be built around each school. Until that is accomplished, a razor-wire fence is to encircle each school. At strategic points around the school, machine gun embankments will be constructed and maned by qualified special forces. As part of the Marshal Law Order, the President will temporarily nationalize all the construction industry so that they can focus their efforts on hardening every school in America.

Entrances to the schools will be restricted. It is suggested that parents have their students at the school entrance no later than two hours before classes begin to give the students time to make their way through the checkpoints. Each of these checkpoints will have a complement of advanced imagining, x-ray, and bomb-sniffing dogs. Rooms will be set aside to strip search suspicious students. Armed guards will patrol outside the schools until school starts. No one will be permitted to enter the school once the doors have been closed. These doors will be hardened, sealed, and on a timer opening only once the school day is over.

No backpacks will be allowed. Each student will be issued a tablet to be used in school. These tablets will not be permitted to be taken home. Parents will be required to purchase tablets for use at home that is explicitly linked to the student's tablet at school. No other device will be allowed to be connected to either of these devices. Should the family not be able to afford a tablet at home, the student will be required to stay at school to complete their schoolwork. The school's gymnasium will be converted into a barracks to accommodate students who cannot go home. Should students have completed their school assignments, they will be allowed to go home on the weekend.

Teacher's pay will be cut in half to pay for all of these changes to the school campus. Teachers will be "nationalized" and required to teach or face imprisonment should they refuse to do so. Those teachers who undergo boot camp and special arms training will be remunerated with their current salaries. They will be issued assault rifles and required to patrol the halls between classes to ensure the safety of the students at school.

All extracurricular activities are canceled. All sports facilities will be converted into a boot camp-style training ground. All students will be required to participate and trained in military tactics and the use of firearms. Guns will not be issued to students, but should the school be attacked, they will be encouraged to pick up their teacher's assault rifles should the teacher be incapacitated during the assault on the school. Those unwilling to do so will be sent to special camps to give them special indoctrination on what it means to be a loyal American.

Soldiers will fan out across the country once the order is signed to implement the President's directive. As new information becomes available, we will keep you informed.

-30-

PREDECESSORS

There has never been a President as great as our current President. If you don't believe me, just ask him. He is quick to state that everything he does is better or greater than anyone who has ever filled the office. No one compares to his ability. To hear the President, all his predecessors, regardless of their party, must have been imbeciles. There is nothing that they could do right, and he has had to fix all the problems created by his predecessors.

It is unfortunate to hear him talking like this because it is simply not true and is not something that we should ever do to those who have gone before us. Those who have struggled to do the job we are currently trying to do, deserve some respect. There is a measure of honor that we should give them regardless of what we thought of their actions. They had a tough job to do, and they did it to the best of their ability. The fact that there is still a country for the President to govern should be enough for us to credit them with doing something right.

If we cannot honor those who have gone before, then what expectation should we have that those who come after us will respect us or hold any degree of honor for us. As the saying goes, what goes around comes around. The President has nothing positive to say about those who have gone before as President. My guess is that those who come after him will have nothing good to say about him. He is digging his own grave and labeling his own tombstone.

But beyond that, this is just not the way we treat people. Not just because we don't want to be treated this way, but because life is challenging enough without people bullying each other. What's more, what kind of example do we give others? What do they see and hear? If, as President of the country, you cannot treat others with a modicum of respect, then the average Joe will wonder why he needs to respect those around him. Come on! Is that the world in which you want to live? Is that the world you want to leave your children? Is that the legacy you want to leave? I would hope not.

BEING PRESIDENTIAL

When the President was running for office, he told the public that he would be the most presidential president there ever was. Of course, this was his hyperbole at its best since he has no idea what being presidential even looks like.

For him, being presidential means that he is in charge, and everyone everywhere does everything he says. Now wouldn't we all want that job? It never happens, and it frustrates him no end. Not only do people not do what he says, they question everything he says, every action he makes, and every decision. This is not what he signed up for.

He signed up to be President of the greatest nation on Earth. He won the election, although to hear him talk, you wonder. He was sworn into office, and now he is trying to be presidential as he understands it. Unfortunately, no one else got the memo, and he continues to rant and rave about it.

One of these days, someone he trusts, I am not sure who that might be, will be able to help him understand what it means to be presidential. I'm not holding my breath that he will listen or even understand how to implement what he is told. It will be so foreign from his way of thinking that it will be as if they are speaking another language. But we can hope.

WHO IS IN CHARGE?

That is a great question. No one seems to know for sure. The President thinks he is in charge and makes a lot of noise, indicating that he is the person who tells everyone else what to do, but some days (maybe even most days) that seems in doubt to those who work in the White House. The President gets up late and has very little interaction with people except through Twitter or the campaign-style stage. He says a lot, but very little of what he says makes a difference.

It looks like on most days that the anchors of Fox and Friends are the ones calling the shots. On other days it seems like the "legacy" media is in charge. And then, on another day, it is those who oppose the President who it appears are responsible for what happens.

You might ask how that is possible. Well, the President watches a lot of television. And much of what he does is influenced by this medium and what they have to say about him. Fox and Friends always say positive things, and the President is constantly quoting them and calling attention to the facts and figures they present. This, regardless of whether those facts and figures correspond to the briefing his top aides and intelligence officers give him.

The information presented on screen is much more reliable, in his estimation, than the information given by his staff. He really does not trust his team, and they all know that. If they say something contrary to what he has seen on TV, they understand that he will look at it with a jaundiced eye and may or may not accept its validity. On the other hand, anything agreeing with his position presented on TV, regardless of its veracity, is accepted without question.

I mentioned that sometimes the legacy media or his opponents are the ones making decisions as to how the day will go. This is because, as some have referred to him, he is a counter-puncher. That is, he cannot take a punch without punching back. Therefore, those whom he opposes can control the narrative as they present the facts because they know that he will strike back.

This plays itself out as the day unfolds. If someone gets under the President's skin, he cannot let it go. It drives him, and he is constantly pushing back. This means regardless of what his staff had outlined for the day, he will be focused on whatever slight or disagreement caught his eye. He cannot help himself. He has to have the last word.

TARIFFS

Every President knows that they get a boost in the polls during wartime. The American public draws together when there is a foe to defeat. Unfortunately, it does not last long, and the poll numbers drop once the conflict is over. This President uses threats as weapons and words as offensive assaults. We have already seen this when it comes to North Korea and even fellow Americans.

The great defender of American sovereignty is at it again by threatening to raise tariffs. The problem is that the President has no clue how tariffs actually work. He keeps talking about the trade deficit in relationship to tariffs as if one, tariffs, are a cure for the other, trade deficits. Unfortunately, it is not that simple, and he will not listen to the unintended consequences which accrue when tariffs are imposed.

The President sees this as a zero-sum game with winners and losers. He is positioning himself and, he thinks, the country to be the winners regardless of what it does to the rest of the world. He claims he is doing this out of a need to protect the "national security" of the United States. The problem is that all he is accomplishing is creating a more dangerous world instead of one where prosperity reigns.

Focusing on the United States' needs to the detriment of the rest of the world is an archaic and self-defeating policy. If we have learned nothing else in the last century, it is that no country, regardless of how big and "powerful," can go it alone. We are all in this together. What happens to one affects all, and what one does to the detriment of the others beggars, everyone.

Tariffs are designed to protect the interest of a country's industrial, agricultural, or technical infrastructure to continue to be viable. Therefore, you create price incentives to keep sectors thriving and sustainable that could not do so on their own against worldwide competition. Consequently, it is essential to protect what is vital and let others do what is not critical.

You can't and really don't want to protect everything. If you spend your energy safeguarding something passé, the world will literately pass you by. Therefore, it's more important to protect your relationships than a particular industry. If someone else can do something better than you, let them do it while developing new products they want and need. This is how to create a larger growing pie that benefits everyone instead of persisting in protecting an old shriveling pie that no one can enjoy.

BASIC FACTS

A news article that crossed my news feed this morning states that the President attacks another company but gets the basic facts wrong. The thought that crossed my mind was when was the last time he got the facts, much less the basic fact, correct. It would seem that every other word, which comes from his mouth is a mistake, fabrication of data, or downright lie. He has virtually no credibility with anyone who follows what is going on in the world.

Therefore, getting the basic facts wrong is not news. It's been there, done that, we are on the merry-go-round again. Let me know when he gets something correct. Then maybe I will start believing he has something worth hearing.

Unfortunately, those he has appointed to Cabinet positions have the same problem. Most seem to white men (and there are not many women or people of color) who under other leadership might do well. There are a few exceptions, and those are the ones who seem to be clones of the President thinking they can do precisely what he does and get away with it. Fortunately, that is not the case in the long run. While the President seems to be exempt from the Law of the land due to his position, no one else in government has that "get out of jail free card."

Sooner or later, everyone, even the President, will be held accountable for their actions and words. But, unfortunately, the country will suffer in the interim. We, the citizens of this great country, are the ones who will have to pick up the pieces once this crew is out of office. All the lies and general mischief they have committed during their tenure will haunt us for years to come. I am not sure some of it will ever be able to be reversed.

In the short run, it looks like we will just need to grin and bear it—woe to us during the next few years.

AMAZON

M r. President, if you were only believable, your attack on Amazon and the benefits it gains from its relationship with the US Postal System would have more of an impact. Unfortunately, you persistently attack all comers, and each attack becomes less and less credible. Pick your battles. Don't just pick on any and everyone who comes along.

First off, sweetheart deals between government entities and business leaders are nothing new. If I remember correctly, you have taken advantage of some of these yourself in the past. It might even be said that your constant use of your properties at government expense is continued abuse of these kinds of relationships. The government has lent itself to this kind of abuse, and, guess what, you are in a perfect position to do something about it.

Instead of railing against your opponents, propose legislation that would limit the kind of abuse you seem to be so opposed to business perpetrating on the government. Of course, you might start with your own companies and set an example for the kinds of relationships that business owners should carry out with the government. In other words, instead of taking advantage of the government through your position as President, you could, at least, make the playing field more even.

As for the postal system, I understand that Congress has a say in their rates. If they are losing money, then these rates should be elevated. On the other hand, some of the reports I have seen indicate that the postal system's purported losses are really a shell game to engender sympathy and encourage Congress to raise the rates.

All of this is to say that a little more transparency and a little less abuse of power would go a long way to helping us, the American public, really know what is going on. This would allow us to support the proposals which could make their way through Congress to address the issues you present. Unfortunately, now what we get is a lot of rah-rah with very little substance. We get a lot of abusive talks and no action. We get a lot of attacks and no victories or change. Isn't it time for something to be done that actually makes a difference?

FACTS

"Don't confuse me with the facts." Or better yet, "I never let the facts get in the way of a good story." These must be the mantras your staff hears daily, Mr. President. Surely, they know better. It would seem obvious that some of them are well enough informed to help you not make such blatant mistakes. The only conclusion is that you don't listen to them. You are so busy watching television that you have no time to listen to the very people who have been hired to keep you abreast of the transpiring events around the world.

You have hundreds, if not thousands, of people who are at your beck and call at all hours of the day and night. Any one of them will answer the phone should you call out to verify any issue you want to rant about. A little fact-checking would do wonders for your credibility, but it would seem that you never make the call. You already know the answers to all the questions and don't need others to tell you what is really happening.

Railing against the caravan of people seemingly making their way to our borders in what you suggest is an attempt to take advantage of DACA is just the latest. They are not eligible for DACA unless you expand the program. It is up to you. What's more, "begging" the Mexican government to stop them at their border seems beneath you and the dignity of the office you hold. After all, you are the President of what is arguably the most powerful country on earth. Should they even make it to the United States, these caravans are still weeks, if not months away. Surely, your administration – Border Security Agencies – should be able to determine how to stop them once they arrive at the border. It would seem that with that amount of time, a plan could be devised to keep them from crossing into the United States.

It's not as if they are making a secret of where they are going. After all, they are traveling in a caravan to protect against elements who would take advantage of lone travelers. Any number of things could be done to track their progress and, thus, know precisely where and when they will arrive at the United States border. Once at the border, appropriate measures can be taken to keep them on the Mexican side of the border.

Come on, do we really need to beg others? Undoubtedly, your administration can develop a better, more proactive solution. (By the way, your wall won't be built before they arrive, so you better be thinking more creatively.)

AUTOCRAT

t is universally understood that the President does not have a background in government but in business. What does not seem to be understood is the kind of business that makes up the President's background. It was not just any business; his background is basically limited to only one type of business. That is, he ran a family business. A mom-and-pop kind of business in which he made all the decisions. That's right, regardless of size, the kind of business in his background is the kind which we find on the corner of many cities in the world. It is run by one person who makes all the decisions.

Therefore, in his world, he was an autocrat. What he said went regardless of the consequences. He did not have to answer to anyone, and it did not make any difference what others thought. If he wanted to do something, he could do it. After all, it was his business and his money. If he desired to run the company into the ground, he could do it, and all evidence point to him doing just that on several occasions, which resulted in bankruptcies.

If he wanted to change the direction in which the company was going, all he had to do was say so, and people responded. His word was final, and everyone who worked for him knew that was true. Evidently, along the way, he suffered very few, if any, personal consequences from running his companies this way. That is not to say that those who worked for him did not have problems; many did. But none of those seem to have affected the President while he ran his companies – at least not outwardly.

There have been, and are, autocratic leaders who run countries much the way described above. Their word is final, and they can pretty much do anything they want to without any personal retributions. Yes, there are consequences which the countries often must pay on the world stage, but the leaders themselves don't seem to be held to account. Russia and China seem to be two of those kinds of countries at this time. Their leaders can say and do almost anything they want, and others respond with approval. Both of these leaders have come up through the ranks and have paid their dues, building loyalties along the way. But, now, they are top dogs, and their word is final.

The President seems to be impressed with both men. The way Vladimir Putin, the Russian leader, carriers himself seem to have really captivated the President. It would almost seem that the President would like to emulate these men. They are his heroes because of what they can do. They do what he would like to do, and he cannot understand why he, in turn, cannot do the same from his position. After all, he is the President of the most powerful nation on earth, and he is the most powerful man in the universe. Therefore, it stands to reason that he should be able to do anything they do, only better.

But America is not an autocratic nation and cannot be run like a mom-and-pop store. The President cannot say, and it is done; there are consequences to what he says. Although everyone understands that the President cannot dictate things done, people still pay attention to what he says because his words are important. The impact they have does not just affect him; they also affect everyone in the country and often everyone worldwide. In other words, while he could run his own company into the ground with only himself and his employees potentially suffering the consequences when it comes to being President, the world suffers.

SPEECHES

Have you noticed how the President gives his speeches? There seem to be one or two things at play, maybe both. Is he too vain to wear reading glasses and has trouble reading what is on the written page? Or is it a new revelation, something he has never seen before?

As you watch him read his speech, especially if he has it on a piece of paper, but even, often, when he is reading from the teleprompter, it would seem that he has never seen these words before. They are entirely new. He seems to be reading them for the first time. Each sentence is read as if it is a stand-alone issue he is trying to understand and with which he is grappling.

Sometimes it looks like he is saying, "Wow, this is good. I wish I had thought that up. Oh, yeah, I'm the one saying it, so I must have thought of it." What he is reading is something new never seen before. I presume this means he does not read over his speeches before delivering them. I would think that his staff would, at least, alert him to the things that he is saying. I understand that he may be so busy watching television and helping TV anchors know what they should be saying and doing that he does not have time for other things, but surely his staff could let him know what he is going to say.

At other times, it looks like he has never seen what he is reading, and he is not a happy camper. He either modifies it or just throws the script away, going off on his own. Which for him is never a good thing. He has a propensity to say the most outlandish things when he does this. Something which often, it would seem, catches his staff totally by surprise. They spend days, if not weeks, trying to "fix" whatever it is he has said.

Finally, there are times he uses the speech as a springboard to go back on the campaign trail. This is where he feels most comfortable. It would seem that his speechwriter artfully includes comfort phrases in his speeches to mollify him as he is presenting the written material. The writer puts in those lines knowing that the President will like them. Maybe this is the writer's way of keeping his job. But it often sends the President off on the campaign trail in the midst of what otherwise was supposed to be a policy pronouncement. And the irony is that the President does not even seem to know it is happening. He goes off on the tangent, happy as a lark, and his audience is left wondering what is going on. The staff comes back to share what should have been saying, and life moves on, or does it?

ELECTIONEERING

t is no secret that the President's bread and butter is being out on the campaign trail. He likes it so much he already established a reelection campaign office and staff just days after the inauguration. Since becoming president, he has scheduled campaign-like rallies in several parts of the country. It is like a junkie on drugs; he just can't get enough of it.

There are reasons for this. Among them is the unfettered nature of the campaign speech. He enjoys speaking off the cuff. In fact, even when his staff prepares well-crafted speeches, he often goes "off script" and says whatever it is that comes to mind regardless of the consequences. It is often obvious from his staff's reactions and rhetoric that they are surprised by what he is saying and are in the process of thinking through what they will need to do to pick up the pieces.

One of the other reasons is that the audience is well-crafted. Select people have been chosen who are known supporters. Critics are not allowed into the arena, although some slip in from time to time. His so-called base is well represented and in full force. They are there to support their man and let him know how much they like him. The cheers and applause are like a drug flowing through his veins, carrying him higher and higher, making wilder and wilder claims and statements.

Of course, when the campaign actually begins, there will be people who will be calling him to account for his words and what he has done. Now he rails against the press for doing that, but during the campaign, members of his own party and the opposition party will take off the gloves, and it may look like a royal free for all.

In fact, I will not be surprised if, during the first debate (even maybe the first public campaign stop, where the audience is not pre-selected), we don't begin to experience something which only he did during the previous campaign. I fully expect those who are debating him to say "liar, liar, pants on fire" when he opens his mouth. Sure, this is a schoolyard taunt prevalent among preteens, but so are the name-calling and bullying tactics that characterize the President's verbiage. This taunt will probably be front and center at all his engagements. Just as he taunted his opponents, not allowing them to speak without the pervasive murmuring taunting he clearly and not so quietly broadcast, I expect his new opponents to constantly assail him with "liar, liar, pants on fire."

Furthermore, because of his lack of credibility and propensity to fabricate lies that serve his agenda, it will be common fare for the general public to mock him at every stop. Those in attendance will shout "prove it" anytime he makes a statement. The other thing I expect to hear is "show us the facts." He claims to know everything and has all the valid information for each of his positions. I am sure that those who oppose him will ask him repeatedly to show his cards and prove that what he is saying is accurate. They will not let him get away with just saying things that he expects everyone to believe just because they came out of his mouth. That will not be enough. He will have to prove that what he is saying is accurate and verifiable.

Unfortunately, this will be very difficult for him because he plays very loosely with the facts and will have no way to prove what he is saying is accurate. It will be interesting to see when the voters, not the media, are the ones asking him to back up his claims. My guess is that we will see fewer freewheeling campaign stops which are not orchestrated. And those that are will have people peppered throughout whose role is to silence those who are taunting him, asking him to prove what he is saying. While there was some of this in the last election, I am sure we haven't seen anything yet as it will be.

TELEVISION

This medium plays a significant role in the current life of the American political scene. This is fitting given that the President is a member of the Television Generation, otherwise known as the Baby Boomers. The latter name was generated by an anomaly in the number of births brought about by the end of the Second World War and culminating with the advent of the Pill. The former name highlights an aspect of technology that has marked this generation. Technology has been a determinant in various generations and may be a better marker than a statistical anomaly such as that described by the name Baby Boomers. The generation before the Television Generation was marked by the Radio. Subsequent generations have been marked by the Computer, Smartphones, etc. Each of these technologies plays a significant role in developing the era involved.

It is amply evident that not only did television play a significant role in the development of the current President, but it continues to do so. While previous Presidents have used television to expand their understanding of the day's events, this President is led and guided by what he sees on television. In the past, Presidents would depend on their circle of advisors for information, advice, and to suggest a course of action the office should follow. On the other hand, this President allows the information he finds on television to give him guidance and only cursorily relies on the staff surrounding him.

While one particular news outlet seems to be his primary source for information and direction, he nonetheless views all of the various outlets. Despite referring to them as FAKE NEWS, he still gravitates to them and often rails against what he sees on them. Those items he finds on these other news outlets, which challenge his narrative, irritate, and often anger him. This anger then degenerates into bluster, name-calling, and often downright provocative actions.

On the other hand, his favored news outlet seems to coddle him and even moderate their news stream to find information that will assuage the President's anger and counter what others tell him. In fact, two aspects of this news outlet are very instructive. It seems to seek information to add credibility to the President's beliefs regardless of how outlandish they may be. The news outlet goes above and beyond to make sure that what they share with the public helps the President. This serves two purposes. One, it gives the President reason to praise this outlet while trashing the others. And, two, because of this presidential support, it augments their ratings and viewership. This latter is significant to the bottom line and may be one of the drivers to their strategy, although they would argue that political beliefs are the drivers.

The second aspect is that the President often uses the material presented on this outlet to set the agenda for his presidency. Therefore, they know it and find it very tempting to channel that agenda. It would seem that they structure their programming in such a way as to drive the presidential agenda rather than just reporting on it. That is to say, the material presented helps set the course for the country, something, which I am sure, gives them great pleasure. It also gives them tremendous power, which may be easy to abuse.

CUTTING OFF HIS NOSE

There is an old saying which says, "Cutting off your nose to spite your face." This is an expression to describe a needlessly self-destructive overreaction to a problem. "Don't cut off your nose to spite your face" is a warning against acting out of malice or against pursuing revenge in a way that would damage oneself more than the object of one's anger.

It would seem that the President has an aptitude for doing the former, and I presume his friends and advisors are loudly shouting the latter. Their cries for restraint don't seem to put a dent in his rushing headlong into creating problems for himself and others, most notably the nation. It would seem that he cannot help himself. He is determined to get back at those he thinks have wronged him regardless of the severe harm it might cause the United States.

Here we go again. The United States Postal System is hanging on by a thread. As he points out, some regulations create problems for the entity and may need to be changed. But the run-up to his directive paints a different picture. It is not the misguided regulations he really wants to change. He wants to undermine someone he thinks is out to get him.

The focus of his ire is a group of journalists who seem to be well connected enough to see and say things before others do. They constantly get under the President's skin by the information they uncover, some of which may be journalist hype, but much of which hits its mark and keeps the general public informed of things this administration would like to hide. This, of course, is why the United States has a free press and guards the First Amendment so arduously.

Rather than present facts which would counter the information these journalists have supposedly uncovered, the President attacks the owner of the medium they use to present their information. Rather than confront the person directly whom he blames for what he purports to be a "smear campaign," the President attacks a deal one of this person's companies has negotiated with an entity loosely controlled by the government of the United States, that is to say by the President himself. What's more, this negotiated deal may be the one thing keeping the quasi-governmental agency afloat.

This brings me back to the first characterization of him presented in this piece. He would rather destroy the United States Postal System needlessly in a self-destructive over-reaction than face his problem directly. He would rather cut off his nose to spite his face than find a solution to the issues he has highlighted.

Yes, the Postal System needs work, but don't use fixing its problems as a ploy for dealing with someone with whom you have a disagreement. Yes, often journalists get it wrong and do not present the facts correctly, but don't slam the profession. Find ways to introduce the information in a way that edifies everyone and advances the nation's best interest.

It's not all about you, Mr. President. In fact, it should not be about you at all. It should be about finding ways to lock arms and move our country forward. It should not be about creating a celebrity but about creating a celebration. It is a celebration of free people freely exercising their rights and being the bright beacon on a hill spoken of by one of your predecessors.

MOUTH

It would seem that the President cannot keep his mouth shut. Regardless of how often people tell him to do so, he just can't help himself. He has to say whatever comes into his mind. Consequences seem beyond him. He does not seem to have any idea that what he says can create immeasurable problems for himself and others. He just has to say what he wants to say.

Those who surround the President have the unenviable task of protecting him from himself. As mentioned elsewhere, his staff is tasked with picking up the pieces and trying to make sense of what otherwise is a totally confusing, nonsensical situation. But his friends and colleagues also must create systems to keep the President quiet and away from the microphones.

This is all but impossible as the media, even favorable media, constantly asks him questions. The problem for those in his court is not that he will be asked a question because they can arrange the questions in such a favorable way to allow him to say things that will help not hurt him. The problem is that he will not leave well enough alone. Once he gets going, there is no stopping him. And once he begins down a path, there is no telling where that path will lead.

This means at times, access to him needs to be limited, though this is impossible given the fact he is, after all, the President. Also making this difficult is the fact he enjoys the limelight and cannot fathom that anything he might say may create difficulty for himself, others, or the country.

In the final analysis, it means cutting him off to limit the damage. Even if he does not see it, others do. Those who have a vested interest in his presidency must do whatever is necessary to keep him from destroying what they, through him, have created. Unfortunately, as mentioned, that is easier said than done.

ASYLUM

Federal law and international agreements call on the United States to protect those who fear for their lives and seek asylum in this country. The President, on the other hand, pandering to his base, calls for the willful violation of said laws. He calls those under his command to prevent those who come to our borders from being allowed to state their case. He calls for States to send National Guard soldiers to the border to block those seeking safe haven from coming into this country. Is it any wonder that others, inside and outside of his administration, flaunt the law? Is it any wonder that those around him and under his command think the law is for others and not themselves? Is it any wonder those who see him abusing the very laws he swore to protect think they no longer are bound by these laws?

Over the course of decades, wonderful people who have found their homeland dangerous have seen the United States as an island of tranquility where they could go should things become untenable. This has been the way we have presented our country to the world. We have told the rest of the world that we have it all together and can show them how to do it if they will only follow our example. We have shouted from the mountain tops how wonderful, peaceful, tranquil, and accepting this land is. Is it any wonder that people around the world have bought into our hype? Is it any wonder they have bought into the concept that this is the land of opportunity like none other, and their fondest desire is to be here?

Unfortunately, not only do those who come, find that the opportunities do not exist, but they find some parts of this country are as dangerous or more so than their own. Yet they still come because they are desperate and desperate people do desperate things.

When the caravan of migrants was making their way north, why didn't the government prepare? Why was our reaction sending troops to throw out the invading women and children? It was no secret where they were going. It was no secret why they were coming. It was no secret what needed to be done to abide by the laws of this country.

Instead of sending troops to the border, we could have repositioned those with the expertise needed to evaluate the pleas of those seeking asylum. It would have been much cheaper and more cost-effective to make sure there were enough agents who had been equipped with the skill set necessary to determine whether, in fact, these women and children were asylum seekers. They could have been processed in an orderly and systematic way to create the least amount of heartache on either side of the border.

But, unfortunately, that did not play into the President's agenda. He needed to create a boogeyman to keep his rhetoric fresh and his barbs pointed. It was essential for him not to take logical logistical measures because that would have been too easy and not polemical enough. So now, the asylum seekers, mostly women and children, sit at the border waiting for their turn to cross while border agents are overwhelmed and in short supply. This allows him to continue the hype and the vehement diatribe. This will enable him to keep the spotlight on himself where he wants it to be at all times.

95

CREDIBILITY

I t is a wonder people in general, and journalists in particular, asks the President anything expecting a straight or believable answer. And yet they not only continue to do so but find it newsworthy when it is discovered that he has lied. Not only that, but his base continues to believe in him, if not him, regardless of the farcical statements he makes.

There is no credibility in anything the President says. Everything he says needs to be taken as a lie or at least an exaggeration. He has no idea what the truth is, and those around him are made to be liars when they repeat what he says or try to back up his assertions. Unfortunately, they have lost credibility because the general public is unsure whether what is coming out of their mouth is the truth or some version of a lie is repeated. It is often the latter since offending or contradicting the President means termination.

The irony is that his own team often lets the cat out of the bag and alerts the general public that the man himself has just exaggerated the facts, misspoke, misrepresented himself, covered over some uncomfortable reality – well, really, he lied.

Because of his lack of integrity, veracity, and credibility, he opens himself and the country to all kinds of abuse. Blackmail, either by a woman accusing him of some misdeed or a national leader wanting to take advantage of the country, is undoubtedly the easiest thing to do in these kinds of circumstances. The President has no idea of what he says because it is incredibly hard to keep track of lies. Nor does he have any idea of what he has done because evidently if you can imagine it, he has done it.

And to top it off, there are more years to go.

IGNORANCE

Could it be that the President is ignorant of many of the things that are going on around him? Could it be that his staff and confidants "fix" things without his knowledge or participation? Could it be that his entourage makes arrangements without him being aware of them? As much as he would like to convince everyone that he is omniscient, it now looks like he is suggesting that things may be done without his involvement.

This raises at least two interesting observations. One, is this an act? Does the President seem to be uninformed to create a possibility of deniability, which could protect him in certain legal situations? This is an intriguing perspective, but it may be giving the President too much credibility. Although conniving, he may not be able to pull this off or even thought of it until someone suggested it. Of course, now that it has been mentioned, this probably will be the spin since it makes the President seem more intelligent than he is.

The other option is that, in fact, his staff may do things to protect him. This would not be unusual and would be the sign of a great team and loyal friends. The problem is that they may do things that create more problems than solutions. They may do things they need not do if they had more confidence in the President.

This, of course, is the crux of the matter. Could it be that given the President's propensity to do things which could create problems, his staff and friends may pay for things for which no payment is necessary or cover up something, which if seen in the light of day, would be proven to be false? This is an intriguing possibility.

The President has admitted being a voyeur (backstage at the Miss Universe Pageant) and groping women (Access Hollywood tape). It is also well documented that he has had affairs, at least with Marla Maples, while married. Therefore, is it a stretch to think that when a woman approaches his staff or a friend with a tale of being molested or having had an affair with the President, those hearing the allegations lend some credibility to the story? Then, as self-respecting friends and loyal supporters, they would be compelled to do whatever necessary to squash the possible unseemly publicity which might come out of this, should it become public. As a result, without even asking the President if it is true, they would turn over thousands of dollars in exchange for non-disclosure agreements.

I am not sure which of these two scenarios to believe. Both seem incredible and totally absurd. But, then, I am beginning to think we might be living in a version of The Twilight Zone. I hope someday we will wake up and realize it was all a bad dream.

LETTING GO

One thing is abundantly clear and obvious about the President. He has difficulty (I'm giving him the benefit of the doubt because it seems impossible for him) letting go of any slight regardless of how insignificant or inconsequential it might be. While others would brush off criticism, ignoring it, the President lashes out. What most people would let slide for the President becomes a huge issue to be dealt with in the harshest terms.

This creates at least two problems. One, every comment, every word, every observation has to be whitewashed so as not to cause the President's ire to irrupt. It would seem that everything causes the President to remember whatever slight he might have perceived or, worse, open up a whole new front. Regardless of what happens, however minor, a new backlash is coming.

Often, he would seem to be shadowboxing. He claims to be a counterpuncher, but in reality, it would seem that he is creating the issue, which then, in turn, gives him cause to punch back. The end result is that everyone around him is walking on eggshells. Everyone in his entourage must measure their words carefully and endlessly to not be caught up in the latest diatribe spewing from the President's mouth.

This brings us to the second problem. It is difficult to get things done under these conditions. The President himself is often distracted and quickly loses focus. Every little thing moves him away from the charted course. And even the charted course often is the problem because he really does not like to be "managed," and he often sees his staff's attempt to keep him on task as "managing" him and attempting to control him.

The staff also finds it difficult to gain traction on any of their tasks. Since they constantly have to "put out fires" or explain things away that the President has said, it takes from their assigned task and prevents them from accomplishing what they are committed to doing. Not only must this be frustrating, but it also must be very tiring. Any time you have to stop doing what you feel is essential to address some trivial and insignificant issue, it drains your energy and causes you to question what you are doing.

Is it any wonder that the best and brightest who joined the White House are leaving? I'm not talking about those who have been caught with their proverbial hand in the cookie jar. I'm talking about those who really make things tick. Those committed civil servants who day in and day out make our government-run. The very best find other more productive engagements, and what we are left with are the mediocre at best.

Mr. President, let things go. Focus on the task at hand. Let your staff help you without second-guessing them at best or ridiculing them at worse. Move on and begin to govern!

PLAYED

Mr. President, you are being "played" like a fiddle. The sad part about that statement is that you make it so easy for those who would want to use you to accomplish their goals to do so. Your ego does not allow you to back down. Your penchant for winning at any cost makes you vulnerable. And your incessant desire for immediate gratification makes you an easy target.

Many leaders on the world stage are master manipulators. This is what it has taken for them to rise to the top of their respective government agencies, and it is what is necessary for them to stay on top. They have honed this skill set and fined tuned it like none other. Niccolò Machiavelli could learn a thing or two from them, and The Prince had nothing on them. It is their way of living, and you, obviously, are out of your league.

You claim to be a master dealmaker, and you may be one in the rough and tumble no holds barred world of American business. But, the business arena has limits and boundaries that are used to give it some sense of order and structure. This is your world. Even when you pride yourself on playing outside the lines or in a real ego boost claiming to draw new lines, you know that you cannot do certain things.

But this is not the world where many of these leaders live and rule. For them, there are no limits or rules. They make the rules, and those rules are constantly changing as they need them to be to accomplish their task. If they do not like something that is done or said, they change it or dispose of the obstacle. Sometimes that means getting rid of the opposition by any means possible.

Not only that but most of these players have a much longer time horizon than you do. They play a long game marked out in years and even decades. While you are pandering to the election crowd gearing up for the next primary or election cycle, they are focused on the rest of the decade or century. What will it take to move into the future is the question on their mind? What will it take for me to continue to stay on top year after year is the problem to be solved. They really don't care about today's vote in Congress or tomorrow's election results. Those have already been set months, if not years before.

This means that you are easy prey for these vultures. They relish when you come to the table knowing full well that they will have no problem gaining what they need from you. They are strategic thinkers who know how to manipulate the "Go" pieces on the board. While they have surrounded you and limited your options, you are playing tiddlywinks and wonder what is going on.

UNINTENDED CONSEQUENCES

When decisions are made, there are two possible outcomes or really two possible groups of outcomes. The intended consequences are those expected or hoped for when the decision is made. This is usually the reason the decision is made. Then there are the unintended consequences. These are the things that happen that were not part of the plan.

Unintended consequences do not necessarily have to be terrible but often then are. We didn't think about these things when we made the decision. In the euphoria of coming to a conclusion about what needs to be done, we often do not think clearly about all of the collateral things that might happen once the decision is implemented. Sometimes this has a happy ending, but often these consequences require remedial efforts to stay another disaster that looms ahead.

As mentioned, intended consequences are the reason the decision was made. As a result of our evaluation of events and circumstances, we have determined this is the best course of action and will result in the best outcome for all involved. While I have painted a bleak picture for unintended consequences, as mentioned, they do not have to all be dreadful.

Should you decide to purchase a piece of land, you may determine once purchased two things. Although you wanted to farm the property, you now find out the plants you wanted to grow on this particular plot will not grow because of the soil. At the same time, you discover that the mineral deposits under the ground are worth many times what you would have received from whatever you might have planted. Therefore, although your intended consequences were frustrated, the unintended ones proved beneficial.

What this means is that we should not take things at face value. We need to evaluate what we think the results of our actions might be and what other outcomes might be possible and what concerns would cascade from those potential consequences. Each one results in something else, which in turn formulates new possibilities. These need to be evaluated until we run out of imagination, otherwise, something will rear its ugly head, and we will get burned.

All of this to say, Mr. President, I do not think that your advisors are helping you think through what you say and do. Or maybe you don't want to listen to them. I don't know if the problem is them or you, but you have a problem. You constantly say things and make decisions without thinking through the consequences of those statements or conclusions. In your mind, they sound good and may even be suitable for what you want to do, but the result is not always to your liking.

This is part of the problem you have with the media. They, by nature, run down all the scenarios and point out all the issues with what you are saying and doing. For you, this is negative press and unwarranted. But if your staff was doing its job, you would have heard all these things before and considered, and discarded them when making your decision. They would be old hat and nothing to worry about because you already took them all into account. You know how it will play out, and you are not concerned about the unintended consequences because the intended one always wins.

Mr. President, do a better job of mapping out all the consequences, not just those you want. Have others outline them for you and help you see what might happen. Then you can just ignore the press as they try to second guess you.

IT'S JUST BUSINESS

Mr. President, it would seem with you everything is just business. The problem is we do not know where your business interest end and those of the country begins. But the impression which comes out of your administration is that your business interest comes first, last, and always. Somewhere in the mix comes the country's interest, but they may be muddled because in your mind, what is good for you is good for the country.

You pride yourself on being a great deal maker but again, what you do makes one wonder who is getting the best deal. Your rhetoric would indicate that you think the United States has received a raw deal in years past from those arrangements made by your predecessors. At the same time, you seem to favor a few (it might actually be limited to a select few). This makes me wonder if you are feathering your own nest and building up your own nest egg.

Of course, given your penchant for secrecy and reticence at sharing any of your personal finances, you leave us no choice but to think the worst. Given your propensity to lie, we cannot take you at your word that what you are doing is best for us. Given those you seem to favor in your deal-making, it makes it even more suspicious. It looks like we are getting a raw deal while you are getting a royal one.

But, of course, it's just business. If the people are gullible enough to elect you as their leader, then they must be willing for you to take advantage of them. You have made no secret that you are the master dealmaker, and as such, you want to make sure those deals favor you. After all, once you leave office, you will need to make the best of what you have done while you have been in office.

You can't really expect your sons to carry on for you. They are not in your same league. They try, but you have always had to come along behind and pick up the pieces. So, it stands to reason that everything you do now is preparing for that day when you will be out of office and back in business full time. I know you can't wait. Then you won't have to play this game of smoke and mirrors. At that time, you will be unleashed to be your very best self, building on the foundations you have laid while President. I am sure you can't wait, but you need to do everything you can at this time to make sure what happens then continues to be great – for you if not for the country.

KNEELING

Mr. President, when did you become the arbiter of what is disrespectful to the flag? What makes you the authority on all things ethical, moral, and of redeeming value in our country? Certainly, it is not your life, the way you treat people, or even the office you hold. Therefore, your objection to kneeling during the National Anthem is ludicrous. The pressure you have put on sports clubs from your bully pulpit is laughable.

Unfortunately, some of your followers do not know better or think that what you say really does matter. They, obviously, are ignorant, or you have totally hoodwinked them. That goes for the sports industry management as well. It is a shame and will only create more division. Of course, this may be precisely what you wish to do because if people are focused on this non-consequential issue, they will not realize that you are not doing anything of consequence anyway despite your rhetoric.

Kneeling has always been taken as a sign of reverence and respect. It is a physical indication of your subjugation to whatever or whoever is the object of your kneeling. Whenever the coach wants to say something special to the team, everyone is instructed to "take a knee." This means taking a particular position and listening attentively because something special is about to be said.

Therefore, when sports players take a knee, two things are happening, neither of which is a sign of disrespect. One, they are being reverent, or, two, they are listening attentively. But in this case, they are also doing something else significant to us and our Constitution. They are exercising their right to free speech.

Bullying, xenophobia, racism, and name-calling are typical fare for you. These athletes are calling attention to the fact that enough is enough, and it is essential to treat people with human decency. Unfortunately, this is not something you are familiar with, and, therefore, anyone who shines a light on it causes you to hit back because you can't stand the heat of the truth.

Instead of calling for a ban on kneeling, maybe we should call for a ban on hateful speech. Perhaps we should call a ban on treating people as inferior. Maybe we should call for a ban on making people feel less than human and of no value. Perhaps we should stand up for those who take a knee and salute their boldness and bravery as they call our attention to the fact that we need to do a better job of supporting and affirming each other.

ERRATIC

Talk about erratic behavior. Up one day, down the next. Talks on hold, now back on. From highs to lows and back again. It gets dizzying reading the White House news. You just never know what is coming next.

Somehow the only person in the whole world allowed to rant and rage is you, Mr. President. If someone else says something derogatory about someone in your administration, you are quick to take umbrage. In fact, the slightest disparaging comment calls for a backlash response that causes the whole world to wonder what is going on.

The irony is that the image of dictators thought to be unhinged comes across as calm and steadfast when placed up against your tirades. Whereas it is expected that the President of the United States will keep the world on an even keel as the leader of the "free" world, that task now has to been borne by others. Unfortunately, it would seem that even those who in other times would have been considered erratic are now thought to be sane.

The markets don't know what to think. World leaders throw up their hands, exasperated. And your followers call for the Nobel Peace Prize.

We are looking for peace, but brinkmanship is what you give us. We seem to be constantly on the edge of some precipice. Even when things look like they are going well, we wonder when the next bomb will fall. When will the next tirade lead to more uncertainty?

Is it any wonder many are concerned we will not even make it until next week, much less to the end of your term?

IF ONLY

A very promising tweet from the President came across my feed stating that he was focusing on the nation and the issues at hand rather than continue to rant and rage against the Special Prosecutor. If only that were true. Of course, lies are second nature to this President, and, therefore, no one takes a statement like this seriously. If only we could believe that he will focus on the economy instead of fearmongering. If only we could count on words of hope rather than hate. If only...

Evidently, this is the way the President has always done business. Every day there is an attempt to scare, intimidate, and in some way coerce those investigating illegal activity. Since he sees himself as the center of this investigation, regardless of the number of times he claims there is nothing to investigate, we can only suspect that there is something there. If there weren't anything, then he would close his mouth, stop the tweet feed, and allow the process to run its course.

Of course, he cannot do this. I don't know if it is because he knows there is something "rotten in Denmark" which he fears will be revealed. Or it's because there is so much wrong; he is afraid some, if not all, of it, will come out. Whatever the case, he continues to cause a bruhaha attempting to make it go away.

It would seem that this has worked in the past. Those who have opposed him or said something or done something he did not like would get a tongue lashing and disappear, allowing him to move forward, crushing all those in his path. If the first lie does not work, then spin a bigger one. If that one falls flat, surely a bigger and bolder lie will work. Whatever it is, a bigger lie should fix it.

I say, evidently, it has worked in the past because he is still at it. I don't have access to any of his private dealings. That's right, no one does because he will not allow anyone to see behind the veil of intrigue he creates. But it must have worked because he has honed it to a superb skill which he uses on all comers.

If only he would get to governing the country and trying to figure out what is best for the nation. But I'm afraid that is not going to happen.

TYRANNY

As mentioned elsewhere, I have lived under the rule of three of the longest-tenured dictators of the twentieth century. Two of these were "rightist" and one a self-proclaimed communist. Whether ruling from the right or left, I found they had several things in common. Unfortunately, I find some of these same qualities in a person who theoretically is President of the world's greatest democracy.

One of the things that became clear very fast is that, in the case of each one of these, their word is final. In fact, no opposition was accepted. As alluded to in the preface, those surrounding the leader discovered early that it was best to keep their head down and keep themselves invisible as much as possible.

These tyrants have all the answers and the best, and personally safest, course of action is to affirm their position and do whatever possible to make that position a reality regardless of the outcomes. Often this means doing things that are at least skirting the law is not downright illegal. But, of course, the President cannot do anything illegal.

At least, that is the assertion of those in his entourage. Since he is the highest legal authority in the country, therefore, although whatever is done by others may be construed as illegal, if it is done by the President or on his behalf, by definition, it cannot be illegal since he is the law. This is ludicrous, but it is the same assertion made by dictators around the world.

Each holds himself (and most seem to be men) above the law because they are the ones who establish what is legal and illegal. If they do it, it is legal for them to do. If they decided that it is illegal for someone else to do it, then it is prohibited until they would like to do it, and then it becomes legal again, at least while they are doing it. Confused. Don't be; just trust that the top dog will do everything right, and you will live a wonderfully peaceful life – especially in some other country.

So, the President is always right; he cannot do anything illegal since he is the arbiter of legality, and if someone has the temerity to "convict" him, he can pardon himself. That seems to sum up the President's arguments except for one thing.

If you have the gall to point out that the emperor (President) has no clothes, then you are, at least until now only, badgered, shamed, belittled, bullied, or in some other way intimidated. Under other dictatorships, whole generations have disappeared. Although maybe not quite as deadly as in those other places, this seems to be happening, at least around the President.

Since the President is the final authority on everything, why does he need anyone else surrounding him and confusing him with the facts or, at least, what they think might be factual? The President, of course, knows better. Therefore, eliminate all those who could obstruct the perfect harmony that the President has designed and allow him and him alone to do it all. Then all things will be great because they will be done the way the President wants them to be done.

RINSE AND REPEAT

Every day is much the same as the day before with you, Mr. President. It reminds me of the instructions on a bottle of shampoo – apply, rinse, and repeat. Mercifully, the shampoo industry only expects you to do it once. Unfortunately, your Twitter feed is repeat, repeat, repeat, ad nauseam.

It makes it terribly dull and blasé for anyone narrating your presidency. Every morning we wake up to the same old same old. That is unless one of your handlers, i.e., the news media, wants you to go in some other direction that day. Evidently, they too get bored with reporting the same things over and over again.

Where are the creativity, boldness, and leadership promised to your followers? Where are the new initiatives that would change Washington, "drain the swamp," and usher in a new era of American greatness? Where is the deal maker who knows how to achieve a better future for the country by bringing about change?

All we have seen is someone bent on undoing whatever his predecessors tried to do. Each so-called initiative is designed to undo something that creative minds in years past sought to use to solve the problems the country faced. The primary role of each of your underlings seems to be to destroy what has been done and feather their own nest in the interim.

But, Mr. President, undoing what others have done is not leadership. Any thug can smash up what others have done. Any bully can belittle and create havoc. Any Neanderthal can destroy what others have made.

Your son has famously stated that your life has become "exponentially worse" since deciding to run for President. If that is true, there is an easy fix – resign. I am tempted to wax eloquently on this, but since I know tomorrow will just be more of the same old same old coming from you, I had better save this savory topic for another exposé.

EXPONENTIALLY WORSE

There is probably a lot of truth to your son's statement that your life has become exponentially worse since deciding to run for President. It takes a lot of courage and fortitude to submit your life to the microscope called politics in America. But as the saying goes, if you can't take the heat, get out of the kitchen.

It is downright astonishing that your son and presumably you were not aware of the difficulties that any President faces while in office. But given your propensity for carping about the abuse you take and the rigorous inspection every little thing you do and say is subjected to, you must not have thought it would happen to you.

I say, astonishing, given the fact that you made your predecessors' lives miserable with your constant barbs and insults. Nothing they ever did was too little or slight not to be subjected to your hyperbole. And if you personally did not rail against something, you encouraged others to do it. As they say, payback is a...

It probably is beyond you since you could not do it before becoming President, but look to your predecessors for guidance. They allowed their detractors, including you, to insult them with impunity while still trying to give leadership to the country. I am sure that they railed and blustered behind closed doors as much as you do about those who criticize every little thing they do. After all, they, too, are only human, and criticism often does get to the best of us. We are trying to do the best we can under the most challenging circumstances, and those outside with little or no knowledge are constantly second-guessing us. It is tough being President when everyone thinks they could do a better job. But they moved on, allowing their critics to bluster as much as they wanted.

Move on, Mr. President. Let the critics say what they will. Allow those who think they know how to do it better to opine all they want. Give leadership to the country and let others deal with your critics.

If you can't do this and you must punch back, nothing profitable or beneficial will come. In fact, if this is what you want to do, you know where the door is located. Use it. Leave and then give voice all you want from the safe sidelines as you did before. As your son so insightfully pointed out, it is much easier to criticize others than to be attacked. It takes a big man to stand up under the blistering carping of those on the sidelines. It would seem that you are not the man for the job. Step down and let someone else carry this burden while you take your swings from the bleachers.

I'M CONFUSED

After the elections, I thought the Republican Party, of which you are the reported leader, gained control of both houses of Congress and the Presidency. In fact, reports are that your party gained a considerable margin. It is also being stated you are the head of the Republican Party, and the party reflects you and your perspective on life and government. All of that to say, I'm confused.

Each morning I read your Twitter feed, and when you're not railing against the news media or claiming the investigation is trumped up, you are blaming the Democrats for not passing legislation to solve the country's problems. Maybe I don't understand how government works. I thought Congress passed laws – primarily by majority vote and the President signed them into effect.

It would seem obvious then if the Republicans have the majority control of both houses, they would pass legislation to deal with the issues the country faces, and you would then have the opportunity to sign them into law. I have also noticed that you have been quite enthusiastically exercising your executive authority and creating your own legislation bypassing Congress, which your party controls. I'm confused.

Who is in control? Am I to believe that the Democratic Party is actually running the show? They are the ones who have control of Congress and the Presidency? They are the ones establishing the agenda and determining what is to be implemented on behalf of the American people?

Are you telling us with your daily lambasting of the Democrats that you don't know how to get things done when you and your party control all the levers of power? Are you telling me that the Democrats know how to get things done, and you need them to exercise their authority to make America great again? Are you telling me that the Democrats are in control despite the polling data? Are you telling me that the Democrats run Congress even though your party is in the majority? Are you telling me that as the President and the majority party leader, you are inept and incapable of accomplishing anything? Is this what you are telling me and the American public? I'm confused.

GOOD

Yesterday, my friend told me that he was glad for all the good the President had accomplished. I was taken aback. Good? What world does my friend live in that he could say something like that? What is he talking about? Am I missing something?

This made me think and realize that maybe I have been so focused on one perspective that I have been totally unable to see life from the perspective of those who support the President. Maybe I cannot see what they see and am ignorant of the good things that have come my way due to this president's actions. Perhaps I need to take a second look at things to ensure that I am not missing something.

Then it dawned on me that part of my problem is that the President's words and life are so loud that I can't focus on anything else. The pain, anguish, and turmoil I see surrounding the President, his party, and the country make me apprehensive about our future. The autocratic nature of many of his pronouncements seems to run counter to our republican values. Therefore, it is hard to see value in what is happening.

As I think about it, I presume that the tough talk, no holds barred, American first and only position the President has taken resonates with those who feel powerless in our modern society. The win at any cost attitude portrayed by the President evidently makes them think he is fighting on their behalf. The zero-sum world in which he seems to live corresponds to their view of life and makes them excited that if someone is going to win, it will be "our side."

The problem is that we do not live in a zero-sum world where there are winners and losers. Unfortunately, the world is a unit where we are all in this together. If someone beggars the other for their own advantage, then everyone loses. The only way to move forward is for everyone to work together to increase the size of the pie, not make their slice bigger at the expense of the others at the table.

Therefore, if we want to win, we need to figure out how to help everyone. The old saying, "a rising tide raises all ships," is more accurate now than ever. The "butterfly effect" has never been more real than today.

Yes, we can celebrate a "take no prisoners" strategy which leaves us at the top of the heap. But, unfortunately, the "heap" will be diminished. Whereas it could be a mountain of prosperity, it will end up being a molehill of depravity.

DEALS

Mr. President, you have indicated that deals are what you do. In fact, you have boasted about being the best dealmaker ever. What I have seen makes me wonder what kind of dealmaker you really are. Obviously, there are deals, and there are deals. Some are more important than others, but I don't think that deal-making is rocket science, although I think you would like us to think it is.

It would seem that from your perspective, the best deal is one you make regardless of the consequences or terms of the agreement. What seems evident is that you like short, pithy non-structured deals. These give you wiggle room and allow you to spin the outcome depending on how the wind blows. In other words, this kind of deal will enable you to take a bow and brag about a win even if the results don't really mean anything.

It's all about the show. If you can look good and make good television, then it must be a good deal. Others, of course, will have to come in and iron out the details. As they say, "the devil is in the detail," but those don't bother you and are really not important. The important thing is that you made a good show, and everyone was happy.

Real-life is a lot sloppier and is full of potholes. That is why you have been able to criticize your predecessor's deals. They were full of compromise. They were real deals that are easy to verify and much more complicated to achieve. Often it takes years to achieve this measure of success. Since you only live in the here and now, there is no way you could ever come up with this kind of deal.

The tragedy is that you have found time to tear up deals that your predecessors achieved. Deals that had taken years to iron out were destroyed in mere minutes to serve your need to show off. Now we will have to wait for a real dealmaker who is willing to pay the price to achieve something lasting and not just a flash in the pan that looks good on television. I am afraid those kinds of leaders are few and far between, as you have so aptly demonstrated by your inability to be one.

RATINGS

The more I watch you in action, Mr. President, the more I realize that the one paramount element in your life is ratings. Here I am not just talking about how many people watch your reality show. I'm talking about how many are engaged in what you are doing. You need to be doing things that will keep people plugged into your show.

Therefore, all the things you do cater to the public and your perception of what will increase your ratings. Substance is of little value. Image is everything, and you are very aware of how people perceive you and what you are doing. As long as your ratings stay up, you will continue doing what you think the people like. If they begin to wane, you will make some other big splash to get them up again.

Each day you check your rating pulse and decide what to do based on what is going on around you. Signing a look-good feel-good mean-nothing deal with a dictator puts you on center stage. Tearing up detailed agreements which took years to achieve keeps the focus on you. Creating chaos with our friends and allies keeps people looking to see what you will do next. You are always focused on your ratings and staying in the limelight.

Even petty things like your feud with your staff and cabinet members play into this agenda. They keep the press talking about you. Despite your feud with the press and claims of FAKE NEWS, you really relish the attention and can't get enough of it. Looking for the leaker at the White House is also an interesting ploy to gain attention when everyone knows they just have to wait until tomorrow's Twitter storm to obtain tantalizing tidbits of gossip and trivia spewing from your office.

There does not seem to be any limits to what you will do to stay in the limelight and keep your ratings up. And, unfortunately for the country, your voracious and insatiable appetite seems to have no limits. The rollercoaster continues as you seek new heights of notoriety. As one pundit put it, "any news is good news, as long as the focus is on me." This seems to be your mantra, and the rest of us are just along for the ride.

TAKING CREDIT

It is impressive; you seem to be doing everything, Mr. President. Or, at least, everything that looks good and could cause people to think well of you. There is nothing for which you will not take the credit if you think it will increase your image.

If the stock market goes up, you take credit. If the unemployment numbers drop, you take credit. If the World Cup comes to the United States, you take credit. If the sun rises in the east and sets in the west, you take credit. Well, maybe you have not taken credit for that yet, but it is probably just on the horizon.

Of course, if the stock market drops ten percent, there is silence from your office, and nothing is said on Twitter. You take credit for the new tax law but say nothing about the fact that you and your cronies seem to be the ones to most benefit from these new laws, while the population at large seems to be left holding the bag.

It seems always to be someone else's fault when things go badly. It's the Democrats' fault when your policy implementations are criticized. It's the news media's fault when the optics aren't what you would like them to be. It's always somebody else.

When are you going to "man up" and take responsibility for problems as well as credit for the good things? It takes a big man to admit that not everything goes well, but you do not seem to be able to do that. You only want good reviews, and anything negative makes you upset. That is a terrible way to live, but it is an even worse way to govern.

THOU DOST PROTEST TOO MUCH, METHINKS!

Others have already highlighted how often you protest the "WITCH HUNT" and have wondered if it is because you have something to hide. I, too, have had that same nagging question circulating, especially since there is almost not a day that goes by that you do not rail against the investigation. Despite your assertion that you would stop mentioning it, that reprieve was short-lived, at best. Day after day, your constant rant, Mr. President, is that there is "NO COLLUSION," and the investigation is all "FAKE." This makes any thinking adult wonder if there is something you are trying to hide by your constant protest.

I have no doubt that your assertion of "no collusion" is accurate, although not for the reasons you profess. Collusion connotes intent to coordinate, which I think would have been impossible given the disorganized state of your campaign. I'm not sure you had a coordinated strategy someone or some entity could have colluded with in bringing down your opponents. In fact, that may be one of the things which undermined the other candidates' attempt to gain the upper hand. They could not figure out what you were doing and, therefore, never could gain an advantage.

Having said that, there is no denying the fact that you invited others, particularly WikiLeaks and the Russians, to undermine your opponent's campaign. Your stump speeches were chock full of such solicitations. But this is not evidence of collusion, just naiveté, ignorance, and gall.

Therefore, I wonder if your protests have another motive. I wonder if they are trying to hide something, not just what everyone thinks. Maybe you are aware of collusion or coordination or conspiracy or perhaps even something more sinister. But more likely, you don't know but don't want anyone searching because you know they will find things you don't want them to know.

It would seem that you are hiding something and maybe trying to protect someone. Obviously, the only ones you really care about protecting are your children, particularly your namesake, so my guess is that they did something, or you suspect they or, more probably, he did something.

The odds are that if, in fact, it is discovered that your progeny was involved in some kind of backroom shenanigans again, it will be because they were, and are, naïve or ignorant. I doubt they knew what they were doing or the repercussions of the things they were doing. They were used. They were played by experts. You know it or, at least, suspect it and don't want the world to know how gullible your family has been.

All this to say that the cover-up is a face-saving ploy so that those around you, your supporters, and the world at large won't know who you really are. Unfortunately for you, the "cat is out of the bag," and everyone already knows that the "emperor has no clothes."

I WANT IT NOW!

As a toddler that doesn't get its way, the President often throws temper tantrums for which the country has to pay. "I want it NOW!" and/or "I want it MY way" may be his two-favorite saying. Although he doesn't always use those exact words, his meaning is obvious in his tone and demeanor.

Given that government is a bureaucracy that runs slow, at best, the President often becomes frustrated, impatient, and irritated. He is not alone, but others have learned how to deal with these issues, not the President. If he doesn't get his way now, we all hear about it, and often the consequences are not pleasant for anyone.

I'll "shut the government down" may be one of his favorite threats because he knows the legislative bodies he has to work with are scared of that prospect. But that is not his only ploy. I'll "impose tariffs," regardless of the consequences. I'll "send in the National Guard," even if there is nothing for them to do. I'll keep scaring, threatening, and intimidating you until I get my way.

Now we have all heard those same kinds of things before if we are parents. Toddlers begin to use them to manipulate us. By the time our children become teenagers, they have honed these elements into a fine skill used every time they don't get exactly what they want.

It would seem that the President is stuck in some "Groundhog Day" childhood loop, which has not allowed him to develop any adult skills. The only way he has to deal with adversity and those who will not bend to his will are those he learned as a toddler.

His staff and those who work for him have tried to channel these impulses and energies in a productive way. Unfortunately, it would seem that even they have thrown up their hands in disgust and allowed the toddler President to have his way. And ultimately, we, the American public, are left to pay the price.

IS IT REALLY TRUE?

Mr. President, the fake news media must be up to "it" again. They are reporting that you have changed your mind. They are telling us that you are backing down. They have the audacity to claim that you are not holding firm. It can't be. Please, Mr. President, put them in their place with your classic vitriolic diatribe. Show them who is the real boss. Let them know that they can't get away with this kind of reporting. Prove to them that you are a strong man and not one who can be pushed around by crowds of crying children.

This is classic fake news, if I have ever heard it. They claim one of your minions is dictating a memo for you to sign reversing course on one of your signature policies. The fake news has gone too far. They claim to have reliable sources that you will sign this travesty once it gets to your desk. I can't believe it.

This must be one of your ploys to weed out those who are leaking State secrets. Obviously, this is a plant you have carefully fed the fake news media through those you have discovered are leaking information from the White House. It would seem that you have found this rat and are now in the process of outing them so that all of us will know the dastardly people who are trying to undermine you and the great things you are trying to do.

This is the only answer that makes sense. Crying children being taken from their mothers would not sway the great President of the United States of American. The sight of children kept in cages is nowhere near the cringe factor necessary to change your mind. Therefore, the reports must be fake. They must be a lie. There is no way they will hold up under scrutiny.

I'm sure that you will come out and tell us what is really going on. You will clarify that this was all a trap, and now the guilty have been caught and given that ultimate notice – You're fired!

MAYBE YOU DO LISTEN, MR. PRESIDENT

Evidently, Mr. President, there is someone out there who can get you to change your mind. I don't know if it is your daughter, wife, or the corner baker who whispered in your ear. It would seem that your heart is not made of stone after all. Someone's deaf touch has tenderized the granite.

Now that we know there is someone who touches you, you better be on guard. Others will take advantage of that soft spot to move you in directions you would never have thought of going. Maybe this is a good sign. Perhaps this tells your followers that you are human after all. Maybe this will help them and others grow closer to you and like you even more than they ever thought possible.

Regardless, this shows the American public that there are people to whom you respond. It could just be a matter of the downward spiral of your image, which was being tarnished by the mothers and children attracting so much attention. Whatever it was, I have no doubt that we have not seen the last of the attempts to get you to modify your position on any number of issues.

Others have tried and have not been successful. For instance, it didn't happen when you saw children gunned down in the schools. But, of course, maybe the border doesn't have as strong a lobby as the gun industry.

Therefore, I am not holding out much hope that things will really change because you think you are on the right track. Regardless of the problems that assail your policies or the difficulties you created, you believe you hold the high ground. You indeed may have the "high" ground because those around you are sinking into a morass of your creation.

But this gives us hope that reason will prevail at some point in the future. My fear is that we will have sunk so far, we will never be able to climb out of the pit.

Only time will tell.

I CAN'T, I CAN'T, I CAN

It would seem that after all of the denials and blaming others for the problem, you had the solution in hand all the time. Over and over again, we heard you say, "I can't solve this problem." Over and over again, we heard you exclaim that the Democrats are the only ones who have the solution. Over and over again, we heard your staff repeat your assertions.

Yet with the stroke of a pen, you changed what had been unchangeable. What are we to believe? Are you as incompetent as you are suggesting? Is your staff so inadequate that they cannot help you see what is right in front of your eyes? Are you going to continue to blame others when you have the ability to bring about the changes?

I guess only time will tell, but if the past is a prelude, it would seem evident that we will face these same kinds of issues again and again in the coming months. You will express your inability to overturn some initiative or policy your administration has implemented. You will exacerbate the problem by refusing to deal with it in an orderly and timely fashion. You will slash and burn all those around you—railing against everyone. But never holding yourself accountable for fixing what you are destroying.

How much will the country have to endure your rampages? How much will the American people have borne the cost of your narcissism? How long will the world tolerate the leadership void left by what at one time was the "leader of the free world"? Unfortunately, only time will tell, and the horizon does not look good.

IT'S A MESS

It's easy to pull apart but hard to put things together. Mr. President, you are very good at taking things apart. In fact, it would seem your minions are masters at this particular skill set. They seem to be able to tear up, tear apart, or destroy what others have done. Unfortunately, they have and continue to have problems creating things and putting things in place which improve what they are destroying.

Pulling apart families is easy. You pick up the child and walk away. Despite the crying, screaming, and pain, you just keep walking. But what happens when you want to reverse course? What happens when you want to put those same families back together again? What happens when you try to find out what happened to the children and try to put them back in the arms of their parents, not so easy, is it?

I am afraid your successors will have their work cut out for them once you are out of office. It may take years to undo the mess you have created. Of course, you may think you will be in office forever. I know you are convinced you and your team are doing a fantastic job. In your mind, all the treaties, agreements, relationships, and families which have been pulled asunder are "building blocks" for the world you envision. Unfortunately for you, the world does not always march to your drumbeat, and you may find creating the brave new world you envision difficult.

Of course, when the world is in turmoil and problems abound, you will claim that it is all part of your grand plan. When children are permanently separated from their families because families cannot be located, you will claim victory against the supposed gangs those children were to become part of in the narrative you have developed. As your Attorney General will no doubt claim, "all things work together for good for those called" to your way of thinking.

This, of course, feeds your narrative because you have always felt that one of your strengths is reorienting the dialogue in your favor. As you pointed out, you can "stand in the middle of Fifth Avenue and shoot somebody" and not "lose any voters." You have convinced yourself of this reality, and the polls would seem to bear you out. Only time will tell what your legacy will be. I know you are convinced you will be the greatest to ever hold the office of President. But legacies can't be spun, they are what they are, and yours may not turn out like you think it will.

BORDERS

r. President, I respectfully disagree with your statement, "We have to maintain strong borders, or we will no longer have a country that we can be proud of" or, at least, your understanding of what that statement means. For almost two hundred years we had "open borders" admitting most everyone who wanted to come into the country. This was true, despite those who, like you, would like to prevent those unlike themselves from coming into the country. It was the very diversity they (and possibly you) were trying to prevent, which has made our country the robust world leader it is today.

The following poem by Emma Lazarus at the Statue of Liberty represents the best of who we think we are as Americans.

Not like the brazen giant of Greek fame,
With conquering limbs astride from land to land;
Here at our sea-washed, sunset gates shall stand
A mighty woman with a torch, whose flame
Is the imprisoned lightning, and her name
MOTHER OF EXILES. From her beacon-hand
Glows world-wide welcome; her mild eyes command
The air-bridged harbor that twin cities frame.

'Keep, ancient lands, your storied pomp!' cries she
With silent lips. "Give me your tired, your poor,
Your huddled masses yearning to breathe free,
The wretched refuse of your teeming shore.
Send these, the homeless, tempest-tost to me,
I lift my lamp beside the golden door!"

I am proud of our country that has welcomed the world to its borders. We are a country of foreigners who have, together, created a bond that is the toast of the world. Unfortunately, all that goodwill is being frivolously tossed away, and we may never be able to recover it.

STRONG BORDERS

Having read my previous section, Mr. President, you probably think that I do not believe in strong borders. Nothing could be further from the truth. I believe strong borders are essential. The conflict arises because I do not think your policies create strong borders. In fact, I believe your policies have weakened our borders, and we will suffer as a result.

A strong border patrol also does not make strong borders. They help keep the peace and serve to help make sure our borders are safe, but they, in themselves, do not make for stronger borders. These incredibly gifted men and women have been put in an increasingly tenuous position by the things you require them to do. It is causing them to find themselves in peril and difficulty, which should not be part of their job description.

Strong borders are made through strong relationships with those countries which border our own. Actually, it is not enough to have strong relationships with bordering countries; it is imperative that we have strong relationships with other countries around the world, which serve as a kind of buffer for our borders. Most of the leadership of the countries (France, Germany, Canada, etc.) with whom you have picked a fight over the course of the last couple of years fall into one of these two categories. Your attitudes and actions make it difficult for them to have our back and help us protect our borders.

It is my understanding that the border between the United States and Canada is the longest unprotected border in the world. This border which stretches from the Pacific Ocean to the Atlantic, is one long continuous easy access from one country into the other. No one, including you, has suggested building a wall along this border. We have not stationed National Guard soldiers on this border, and our border patrol officers are few and far between. And yet, this is a very strong and secure border. Have you asked yourself why?

I think the reason this border is so secure has nothing to do with the common heritage which some people on both sides of that border share. That is equally true of the border between the United States and Mexico. I think it is due to the high regard we have always held for those who live in that country. Unfortunately, we have not always held those who live along our southern board with the same level of respect.

It is imperative that we back off the rhetoric of blame. It is time we look beyond hiding behind barriers and create doors and bridges which will help all the people, both north and south, learn to live, work, and prosper together. It is time to stop name-calling and seek to care for each other. Only then will we begin to discover ways to live together and triumph. And that will give us strong borders.

RED HEN

The United States has come to a difficult time. Civility seems to have disappeared. We find it difficult to treat each other with any courtesy and understanding. It appears that only those who agree with us are acceptable to us.

The business which asked your Press Secretary to leave, Mr. President, did wrong. It is a public establishment, after all. As far as I know, she was just eating a meal. She was not putting on a political spectacle. If she had, it would have been acceptable for the owner to ask her and her group to leave.

Other members of your staff have been harassed at meals or in other public establishments. People, some in public office, have called for others to be offensive toward those in your entourage. This is wrong!

Unfortunately, Mr. President, you have reveled in this same kind of activity. You have called your followers to abuse others and have even invited your staff to be abusive. Some claim that all of this being discourteous began with you. I doubt it because I am sure that others long before you ever made an appearance have also been uncivil and have used it to their political advantage.

You, though, have popularized it at this time and seem to have given those who follow you the freedom to be not only rude but also cruel. Now this discourteous behavior appears to be coming home to roost. Your team, now, is the brunt of other's ill-mannered behavior.

This needs to stop. We need to be more courteous and less impolite. We need to learn to tolerate those who disagree with us. We need to value other people's opinions. We need to recognize that it is alright for people not to agree and understand that we can disagree without being disagreeable.

REVELING

It would seem that other people's misery brings you great pleasure. Time and time again, your tweets point out how others have failed or have done something wrong. Regardless of how contrite they might be and even when they apologize to you and others, you seem to think it is imperative that you highlight their misery and point out their foibles.

Of course, since you are perfect and have never done anything wrong or for which you need to apologize, you would not understand those of us who have those most human of failings. To err is human, and everyone does something for which they are sorry at some time or other. Even though you think you are perfect and have never done anything wrong, that is not the case. You, too, are human.

Calling people out when they have done something wrong might be a noble venture when what they do causes great harm to others. Beating someone up for an error when they have already admitted to the mistake and apologized for it is bullying. You, Mr. President, are a bully.

The world is full of too many bullies. It doesn't need a bully-in-chief which seems to be what you think is your calling now that you have become the President. We all fail. We all make mistakes. We all have problems. We all do things we should not do.

What the world need is grace. We need to treat each other with kindness. We need to look for the best in people. We need to seek out how to help and not hurt.

I try to be fair in this collection of comments. I have even tried to give you the benefit of the doubt. I will try harder to give grace. Unfortunately, you often make it difficult to do so.

SUPPORT OUR LAW ENFORCEMENT

Your call for support of ICE is refreshing. We should support all our law enforcement agencies. In fact, we should support all our governmental bodies.

This does not mean that we can't question decisions some of them make. It also does not mean that we cannot speak out about the conduct some of them exhibit. But it does mean that they should not be ridiculed, derided, scorned, or in some other way belittled. They are all doing tough jobs under often very thankless circumstances.

I am sure that ICE knows that they are the cause célèbre of the moment, and should things change, you will change your tune. You have been very wishy-washy, unreliable, and so often changeable that most of us have whiplash from trying to follow your tweets. ICE is aware that you will begin heaping ridicule on them sooner or later, just like you have on so many of their colleagues in law enforcement.

The irony is that you, as President, command so many of the agencies which you disparage. They follow your instructions and are doing the very best they can within the guidelines laid down by the law. If you do not like what is happening, don't call them names.

Your disdain is painful for us who watch on the sidelines. I can only imagine how much it must hurt those who day after day lay their lives on the line.

Your role is to give direction, not derision. You are to give hope, not heap scorn. You are to help them, not hurt them, which is precisely what I am afraid is happening.

As you pointed out in your tweet, they are on the front lines against some very "bad people." ICE is not the only one serving this purpose. And yet, I have no doubt that those very same "bad people" gain encouragement from you. They probably think that if you hold those charged with apprehending them in such low regard, why should they respect them.

There's that word – respect. All aspects of the law enforcement community deserve and need our respect. You, too, should respect them. Once those "bad people" see we are united in our support and respect, they will be less bold at going up against these fine men and women who each day try to keep us safe and make sure these "bad people" are behind bars where they belong.

ADULATION

We all need people to brag about us from time to time. We need people to think well enough about us; they will share some incredible detail of how great we are. It is part of our human nature to want people to think well of us and to share those thoughts with others.

This is obviously important to you, as demonstrated by your Twitter feed. Whenever you become aware of someone saying something nice about you or supporting a position you have taken, regardless of how arcane it might be, you jump on the tweet and repost it. Some days your Twitter feed is one retweet after another as you shine a light on those who have said nice things about you.

I dare say that many of those who say nice things about you hope you will repost their tweet. It is their way to gain some national notoriety. A relatively unknown says something you like, and suddenly their Twitter feed becomes the talk of the town, and their tweeter followers multiply. That is not a bad strategy for someone wanting to increase their numbers and tweeter followers. It makes me wonder about the sincerity of some of this adulation. It seems somewhat self-serving on their part.

You, though, do not seem to be able to wait for others to find nice things to say about you. It would seem it is essential for something great about you to be found on your Twitter feed each day. Therefore, amid your ranting about the Special Investigation, the Election results, the Democratic Party, etc., you insert from time to time some bit of self-adulation. It need not be true; it just needs to appear on your site.

I guess it falls in the same category as lies and the expression coined by Adolf Hitler when he dictated his 1925 book *Mein Kampf*, about the use of a lie so "colossal" that no one would believe that someone "could have the impudence to distort the truth so infamously." And then regimented by Joseph Goebbels in his famous quote: "If you tell a lie big enough and keep repeating it, people will eventually come to believe it. The lie can be maintained only for such time as the State can shield the people from the political, economic, and/or military consequences of the lie. It thus becomes vitally important for the State to use all of its powers to repress dissent, for the truth is the mortal enemy of the lie, and thus by extension, the truth is the greatest enemy of the State."

WRITING

I t would stand to reason since you do everything superbly well, then your writing should be spectacular. Evidently, you have been bothered by those who have called attention to the mistakes you make on your Twitter feed. Frankly, I am trying to understand the tweet.

On the one hand, you brag about your writing skills. The evidence you give is the book I understand made the bestseller list. Although I wonder about the authenticity of the brag. First, I know you had the assistance of a ghostwriter. A ghostwriter in and of itself does not mean that you are a poor writer, but the general perspective is that utilizing a ghostwriter would indicate that you really did not write the book yourself. You provided the stories. You gave the writer the details for the book. But it was the ghostwriter who crafted the final product and created the best seller.

Of course, your argument probably is that the book is a best seller because it is about you. I would not question that argument. In fact, I think that is precisely the case. Given your notoriety and fame (some might say infamy), it would have been surprising if a book about you did not make it to the bestseller list. Particularly since you have been in the public limelight and, more currently, in politics.

However, that does not make you a great writer; it just makes you someone about whom people are interested in reading.

That brings us back to the Twitter feed. I, too, have noticed a general trend of poor grammar and misspelling, not to say anything about hyperbole and fiction. But I don't think that a Twitter feed indicates the level of writing a person can produce. This is due to the medium. It is not conducive to great writing. It is generally off the cuff and reactive as opposed to well thought out and deep.

Therefore, I would not think that your Twitter feed is any indication of your skills. To me, it simply is an indication of your humanity and the fact that you are one of us, capable of making mistakes. Of course, given your penchant for perfection, that might be too much for you.

FIRST AMENDMENT

Among other things, the First Amendment to the Constitution of the United States guarantees its citizens the right of free speech as long as it does not infringe on someone else's rights. It is one of the tenets which has made America great. With it, Americans have been able to express their opinion without worry that reprisals will come as a result of what they say. We have even protected those with whom we disagree because it is their right to express themselves.

That does not seem to be the case at this time. When someone says something with which you disagree, Mr. President, you not only are quick to point out their error but also to ridicule and mock them for having said it. No slight is too small. No comment too insignificant. They all are met with scathing criticism, which is unwavering in its harshness. It is almost as if you believe that you are the only one who has a right to express an opinion. No one else has that privilege. It is reserved for you and you alone.

There have been other times in the history of this great country when those in government used their bully pulpit to control those who would disagree with them. The McCarthy era comes to mind when everyone was painted as a Communist and would be lambasted or worse. People were hurt, and many lost their livelihood, and some even lost their lives due to one man who thought he was above the law and could bully people regardless of the rights supposedly protected by the United States Constitution.

It was a sad day in our history. My plea is that we learn to be civil and allow even those with whom we disagree to express themselves. There might be something we can learn from them. They may have something to say we need to hear. No one, not even you, Mr. President, has all the answers. Historically, that is one of the things that made this country great. We listen to each other's opinions and then draw together the best ideas to develop a solution that works best for all.

YOU REALLY KNOW HOW TO PICK 'EM

The quality and character of the people with whom we surround ourselves says a lot about us and our own character. Over and over again, those people whom you have selected to lead various agencies and departments have left with a cloud hanging over their head or worse. It makes one wonder about the person who picked them for the positions they held.

Of course, you may not be to blame for their foibles and failings. After all, these are fallible people, as we all are. There does not seem to be any suggestion that you caused them to act the way they did, but it does call into question your ability to pick people capable of leading the various elements of government.

Some seem to have had no scruples whatsoever. They seem to think that the government's money was their own to do with whatever they wanted. Lavish spending on things that add no value to their job or seem to have any reason is just one of the issues that have come out regarding some of these people.

Some seem to be over their head. They sit in the room with people who are several times richer than they are and do not know how to handle their surroundings. They rub shoulders with people who have impressive portfolios and who had run successful companies. They evidently feel inadequate and need to compensate by surrounding themselves with accouterments of the rich and famous. These trappings might be impressive elsewhere but simply look like exploitation in the hands of these naïve and sometimes immature men and women.

Even those with generous financial portfolios seem not to know what to do with the trimmings which come from leading a government agency. They are so used to everyone playing up to them that they do not seem to know what the words "servant of the people" mean. It would seem in their minds that others are the servants, and they are the masters.

Still, others seem to have come into office with an agenda. I know this is true of every new officeholder and will continue to be true long after you are gone. Unfortunately, this crew does not seem to mind who they hurt or what damage they do in the meantime. They feel that they have been given the mandate to run roughshod over everything and everyone that stands in their path. You seem to have set the tone for this and even have blessed their efforts with commendations and accolades.

Others do not seem to have any moral foundation. Their past, speech, and actions seem to show a total disregard for others or the nation. Someday there will be an accounting for them and you. I wonder how each of you will stack up with the luxury of hindsight. At least, as of now, it would seem that history may not be as generous to you as your followers are now. Only time will tell. In the meantime, we have to muddle through, hoping for the best.

A MILE WIDE...

The saying, "a mile wide but an inch deep," seems to be an apt description of you and your team. Another down-home saying which might be used is "all hat and no cattle," but regardless of whether it is stated formally or informally, the message is clear. There is very little substance in what you say; it is mostly for show.

Your stump speeches don't have much to say. They are basically designed to inflame and manipulate your supporters. They are full of platitudes, hyperbole, and fallacies at best or downright lies at worse. You seem to never tire of taunting, ridiculing, or simply bullying those who disagree with you.

Even subtle attacks (and some not so subtle) of the #MeToo movement is not beyond you. Given your past history with women, this should come as no surprise, but it shows that you have no filters and really no idea of how crude and little you show yourself to be.

When you have prepared speeches that you in turn read, they come across as stilted and insincere. Your reading style is so painful to observe anyone hearing you has difficulty focusing on your words due to your delivery. There may be something of substance that needs to be heard, but who can hear it given how you present the material?

You claim to be an intelligent person; therefore, I can only surmise that all of this is done on purpose. You don't want to say anything. You simply want to hear yourself talk and need those who support you to continue doing so.

That is too bad. We need substance. We need concrete direction. We need leadership. Step up, Mr. President. Lead this country, don't continue trying to snow us with superfluous words inundating us with bologna instead of substance. The American people deserve more, and they are expecting you to provide it.

SAY ONE THING, DO ANOTHER

It is evident you want people to think you are a man of your word. At least, you want those who attend your rallies to believe you do what you say you will do. It would seem you understand that this perception is critical to you staying in command of your supporters.

Unfortunately for you, there seems to be a growing body of evidence that you are more show than go. You talk a good talk, but your walk does not correspond to your words. In other words, what you are saying to your base is, "Do as I say, not as I do." This does not work very well for parents, although many try, and I don't think it will work long term with those who have put you in power.

Sooner or later, those who have been your backers will grow weary of you saying one thing and doing another. You say that you want to hire Americans, although it would seem that some of your companies scour the help wanted list for foreign nationals to bring aboard. Of course, you have said that you want the best and brightest to be granted immigration status into our country. Your supporters may wonder about your America first verbiage, and weren't there any best and brightest Americans already here who could have been hired.

Of course, it would seem that many of those hired are not those who would be granted special visas, but Hispanics. I presume that all of them are legal since it would be terrible for ICE to raid one of your establishments and catch undocumented workers at work. Although I have heard anecdotes of undocumented aliens building the very detention centers where other undocumented illegals will be housed. The irony does not pass them by.

It would seem that your rhetoric ridiculing Hispanics and calling attention to those who are here illegally keeps this population group on edge, fearful of their future. The more you talk about it, the more scared even those born here have become. Even those whose families have been in this country longer than yours; find themselves under suspension.

I wonder if this is your way of keeping your workers "down on the farm," so to speak. By keeping them scared, you can keep their wages low. By making them the focus of your derision, you can keep them from speaking out. You can keep your cost down and your workers pliable.

But that does not seem to be the only egregious failure of your actions to live up to your rhetoric. It would seem your companies also tend to bring products from overseas instead of buying American-made products. In both cases, workers, and products, you, I am sure, see yourself as a smart businessman. But what about the other intelligent business people you have ridiculed over the years?

Will those who support you finally see how two-faced you are? Will they eventually turn on you, abandoning your bandwagon out of disgust and disillusionment? When that time comes, it will not be a pretty picture. I don't think you can keep this up long term, but I do believe you have convinced yourself people don't care. They just want you to keep them entertained. I think you will find that is not the case, and sooner or later, you will pay the price for your arrogance.

BUSINESS FIRST

Whereas most of your rhetoric would indicate that you want to put "America First," your actions belie that effort. Actually, what your policies and the processes carried out by the various governmental agencies under your team's leadership show is that you have narrowed that message down very finely to read "American 'Lobbies' First."

It would seem evident from recent actions that your team is very responsive to the lobbyists who have infested the swamp you vowed to drain. On the surface, this would seem to be an effort to put the interest of the general American public ahead of the rest of the world, regardless of the consequences. At least that is what the hoopla coming out of your mouth, and your spin machine would have us believe. But as one digs deeper, you realize that you, Mr. President, have no interest in the general population. They are pawns to be sacrificed when needed.

Business takes first priority, and more importantly, companies you perceive support you. Maybe even more specifically, business interests that support you personally, but that is difficult to prove given the veil of secrecy covering your personal finances and those of your associates. Regardless it is evident that the lobbyists have you in their back pocket, and you dance to their tune.

Two things make this alarming. One, the American public is paying a hefty price for you kowtowing to the lobbyists' agenda.

Second, the United States is withdrawing from the world stage and abdicating its role as a world leader. As a result, Russia and China are stepping into the gap and taking over. Either one would be a calamity. Both are a world catastrophe, and you seem oblivious to it all.

The void you are leaving on the world stage by your "America First" is playing right into their hands. They are in this for the long haul, not just the next quarter. And I'm afraid you will not even know the danger you and the United States are in until it is way too late.

WORLD STAGE

When you won the presidency and took up the mantle of President of the United States, you also walked out onto the world stage as the supposed leader of the free world. This was your right as won in hard-fought battles by your predecessors and at the cost of many American lives.

As you meandered through the hallways of power around the world in various meetings, it was your understanding that those from other countries would defer to you because of your position as President. And defer they did. They did so because they, too, understood the place you had assumed and have been more than willing to allow you to take your place as first among equals. They would even allow you to physically push them aside as you made your way to the front of the line.

But the luster has worn off. Leaders around the world no longer are deferring to you. Positional authority will only take you so far and then, if not augmented by authentic leadership skills, begins to wain and eventually fade. Yours is quickly waning, Mr. President. You no longer are held in the esteem of which your office is accustomed.

Mr. President, it would seem that you think you have things under control. You think you know how this game is played. Unfortunately, for the most part, you come across as nothing more than a schoolyard bully without a clue about what is going on around you. The leaders of some of these countries are seasoned professionals with years of dealing with those within their own infrastructure who think that might makes right, as you seem to do. They have used them until they are no longer useful and then moved on. You are simply another hurdle in a long line that they have already overcome.

They are in the midst of passing you by. Soon you will be an afterthought as they move on to take charge. The void you have left on the world stage will be filled by others. Nature abhors a vacuum, and you, Mr. President, have left a leadership vacuum which others will fill much to the detriment of this great country. You have put us at a disadvantage and have hurt our future. Hopefully, others will be able to come behind you and repair the damage before it becomes permanent and irreparable.

CONTEMPT

This is the word that comes to mind when I think of how you treat those around you, especially the American people. You have no respect for anyone other than your chosen few. This is especially true as I think of those often referred to as the "little man." Those at the bottom of the food chain.

I am sure in your mind there is a reason they are at the bottom and have not moved up. It is obviously their ineptitude that has kept them down. If they were as skilled as you are, then they would have achieved great success. They are to be pitied but not taken into account when making world-changing decisions. They really don't count.

In your mind, it would seem, if you are not a titan of industry, a man of means, then you really are nothing. I use the term "man" on purpose because I am not sure you have any respect for women. They, too, are just instruments to be used and discarded when something better comes along.

For all your vaulted rhetoric supporting the "common Joe," I am not sure that you have a very high regard for the average worker. In fact, I am not sure you have ever had a meaningful conversation with any of them. Of course, you may not have had a meaningful conversation with anyone other than yourself, given your egotistic personality.

This is too bad because, despite your confidence in the billionaires with whom you have surrounded yourself, it is the average Jane and Joe, the common man and woman who have made this country great. Yes, the history books only highlight the lives of the great titans of the past, but they would not have achieved anything if it had not been for the backbreaking, mind-numbing blood, sweat, and tears of the millions of ordinary workers who have put this country on the map.

Think about them the next time you make a decision. See how your tirades affect them. Look into how your decrees change their lives and make them harder. "Walk in their shoes," at least for a moment, so that you can begin to understand the sacrifices that have taken place to allow you to live the life of comfort and privilege you flaunt so carelessly.

NAÏVETÉ

Mr. President, most days, I just stand amazed at the things which come out of your mouth. Unfortunately, that is not a compliment. I wish that it were, but the things you say cause me to cringe and wish that I had not heard them.

The other day, someone questioned you about your meeting and agreement with the President of North Korea. You explained that you had a contract with him and had sealed it with a handshake. Really, Mr. President, can you be that naïve?

I thought you were a savvy businessman who had earned his chops in the construction industry in New York and New Jersey. Now, admittedly, I do not know anything about what goes on in that environment other than what is reported in the news, movies, and television. These reports seem to indicate that this is a hard place to work, and the people there are really tough. You seem to allude to this during your campaign, substantiating your credibility as a deal maker because of your background in this arena.

I took this to mean that you knew how to play hardball and were not afraid to throw a few punches when necessary. The rough and tumble world of unions and construction, you indicated, had been a great training ground for you and gave you the background required to become President. I am beginning to wonder if this is really true. Either that area is hyped up by novelist and the fake media, or you really didn't learn anything there.

What you signed was an agreement, not a contract. You have spent years pointing out how governments, including North Korea, have hoodwinked previous administrations and have not lived up to their agreements. What makes you think that they will abide by what you have said? Oh, yes, you shook hands. That makes all the difference in the world. No one could ever betray a handshake.

Grow up, Mr. President. I am sure that the President of North Korea knows your infamy for lying. He knows that a large part of what you say is hyperbole at best, if not pure fiction. He probably thought that since you lie all the time, it was alright for him to do so. His father and grandfather had lied to previous administrations. He knew you lied. What's the big deal? You had a good time. He got you to agree not to hold any more training exercises. He got the spotlight on the world stage. He is now playing with the big boys. What more could he want?

Wake up, Mr. President. He got everything; you got nothing. Now he is ready to get back to the business of keeping control of his county. I'm sure it's nothing personal, Mr. President. I'm sure he didn't mean to offend you. His handshake was probably sincere. He meant it at the time. Now reality has set in, and it's time to get back to work. After all, he has a country to run, as do you.

Hopefully, you have learned something and will not go so blindly into your next meeting. But I have my doubts. As we saw with the President of Russia. I'm sure you had a great time. You seem to be making some wonderful new friends. At the same time, you seem to be throwing those who have stood by us historically overboard. Maybe your new friends will be there for you when your term ends. Perhaps they will continue to greet you warmly and remember the great handshakes when you no longer have the bully pulpit you so ignobly utilize with our allies and friends. Maybe they will be your friends because they have never been very friendly to the rest of us. But then we are all just pawns you cast aside when you no longer need us.

ZERO-SUM GAME

Mr. President, it would seem by your actions and statements that you believe we live in a zero-sum world and that you are playing a zero-sum game. My observations are that nothing could be further from the truth, and it is when people and countries act this way that the world becomes poorer and worse off.

The dogma your actions convey loud and clear is that if someone else is winning, you are losing and vice versa. Therefore, you always have to put someone else down. You always have to be knocking out the competition because whatever they gain is your loss. It would seem, from your perspective, the only way up is on the backs and heads of those around you. Your ladder of success is the bodies of those you've vanquished. That is a deplorable way to live life and one that beggar's humanity.

We do not live in a zero-sum world. And when world leaders of the present and past, including our own Presidents, have governed this way, the world ultimately is the loser. Most wars have been fought from this premise, and your current trade war is no different. Unfortunately, when everything is over, and the white flags have been raised, everyone "winner" and "loser" ends up losing. There are no winners in a world with a zero-sum mentality.

The United States was built on the concept the "sky is the limit," and the "pie is always getting bigger." These are foundational perspectives that have allowed us to move forward as a prosperous nation. We have prided ourselves, thinking that American ingenuity, skills, and hard work can overcome any obstacle which would get in our way. What's more, our whole structure is built on the principle that we can do all this together. What the US military famously calls "no man left behind."

We are all in this together, and it will take all of us working together to make the world a better place. Just because one person is successful does not mean another loses something. Success breeds success. That is one reason so many people from around the world want to be part of this great nation. They want to have the freedom to be all they can be (borrowing a slogan from the Army).

It's all right for other countries to succeed and move forward. It's alright for us to have an imbalance in trade as we move to the next great thing. As the world's economies improve and we develop newer and better things, they will want what we have. But if we constantly put others down eventually, we will all be dragged down because no one will be able to move forward. No one wins a war, trade, or otherwise. Everyone loses. Only as we unite our forces and move forward together can we become what we were meant to be.

DRAIN THE SWAMP

During your pre-election stump speeches, you famously talked about draining the swamp in Washington, D.C. You explained that corruption flowed freely in our nation's capital and that it would be your job to get rid of those who were bleeding the country dry. You would tell them, "You're Fired!"

People applauded and approved of your message. They were tired of the politicians who seem to be in the back pocket of some lobbyist or other. They were disgusted by the incompetence and ineptitude they perceived, which flowed freely down the corridors of power. They wanted to cut out the waste and bring balance back to our legislative process.

Mr. President, since you have been in office, there do not seem to be any swamps that have been drained. In fact, it appears from my observations that not only has the swamp remained, but, in many ways, it has gotten larger and swampier. Whereas in the past, we only had to deal with crocodiles and alligators. Today, though, we have to deal with sharks, crooks, abusers, and a whole series of other contemptible personalities in addition to the crocodiles and alligators. You have surrounded yourself with people of questionable moral standards, and those few people of integrity who have made it on board are getting out as fast as they can.

I'm wondering if, instead of building a wall on the Mexican American border, we would be better off building one around Washington, D.C. This way, we can keep the riff raft inside and allow the rest of the country the freedom to do well without having to deal with the graft, greed, pettiness, abusiveness, lies, and moral failures which seem to characterize so many of the people on your team. Given the pictures, I have seen it wouldn't have to be as tall and, therefore, not as expensive as the one you have proposed. I say this because of the large frames many of these men have from all the gourmet meals they have enjoyed at taxpayer's expense. I know the lobbyist garner their resources from special interest groups, but I can guarantee that the taxpayer is ultimately paying the bill regardless of what it says on the business card.

Of course, we would have to set up a checkpoint and develop a robust wall security system because I am sure there would be those inside the wall who would want to get out to practice their wares on the innocent people who make up this great land. Draining the swamp looks impossible. Therefore, let's just seal it off so it will stop creating problems for the rest of us.

FRIEND OR FOE

It has taken me some time, Mr. President, but I think I am beginning to understand your nuanced personality. Particularly as it comes to seeing others as "friends" or "foes" or, as you might prefer to call them, "collaborators" or "competitors." This is still a work in progress as you rile the nation and the nations, but a picture is forming.

One of the nuances of this whole issue is that I don't think you have any real friends. You have people you use. There is family. And then there are others. Some of those you use or who fit in the other category may think they are your friends, but when the time comes, you will move on, and they will be left behind.

You see yourself as a self-made man. You think of yourself as having "pulled yourself up by your own bootstraps." This is not reality. You came from a very privileged position and had numerous advantages which others, even in your circle, did not have available to them. But this is the way you see yourself, and you see others who have not been as successful as you, as inferior. They are there merely to provide whatever assistance you should need. They are at your beck and call.

You seem to admire those who have power, particularly those who can use it with impunity without seemly having to render accountability to anyone. Those who hold a dictatorial rule over their countries seem to be in this category. You would like to be able to do what they do but feel thwarted by the checks and balances inherent in the democratic system. In fact, you see these checks as a severe weakness to our system.

This is one reason you seem to hold the other western leaders in contempt. You see them as weak. They are beholden to special interest groups or morality, which inhibits their ability to act with the license you admire. They are dependent on other people or other countries, which makes them weak. Only the strong can act independently without accountability, or at least that is your understanding of the world as it should be.

Therefore, in the final analysis, there are no friends or foes, collaborators, or competitors. There are only the strong and the weak. And you hold nothing but contempt for those whom you perceive as weak.

HAND IN OUR POCKET

As you have talks with world leaders and deal with those seeking refuge in this country, an interesting phenomenon presents itself which says a lot about your character, Mr. President. You don't like anyone who you think has their hand in your pocket. In other words, you get upset at anyone, or any country you think is taking what is rightfully yours. Anyone you perceive as taking advantage of you is someone who needs to be set straight in the harshest of terms and as quickly as possible.

Immigrants are subject to your ire because they benefit from a privilege you don't think they deserve – living in the United States. They have not paid their dues. They were not born here. Although some were born citizens of the United States, you also don't think they deserve that distinction; that may be a race or economic status issue. You perceive that those crossing the border illegally (and it's almost impossible to gain permanent legal access to the country) are demeaning the country. They are stealing your birthright. They have their hand in your pocket, and you don't like it.

European leaders have, often gladly, allowed immigrants to enter their countries. There, therefore, must be something terribly wrong with these world leaders. They must not love their countries like you love yours. If they did love their country, they would not allow this riff-raff to take what is rightfully theirs. Obviously, they must be weak.

Not only that, but countries around the world are taking advantage of the United States. We have to protect them at a high cost to ourselves. There are seemingly substantial trade imbalances. They are taking our jobs away from us. They have their hands in our pockets.

Of course, the only thing that matters in these transactions is the bottom line; the intangibles, which accrue to the United States due to these agreements, don't count. It is only the bottom line that matters, and we are losing. And the bottom line is that they have their hands in our pockets.

CRASS HUCKSTER

There you go again, Mr. President, hawking your wares and trying to advance your personal brand. This should not come as a surprise to anyone since you have been doing this from the very earliest days of your campaign. You don't seem to be able to control yourself.

Much was made about your campaign parties and the blatant hyping of products that bear your name. Promoting your brand is what you have always done. This is the actual product you sell, and it evidently has been quite lucrative. Therefore, I guess it should not come as a surprise to see you continue doing this even all these months later, well into your presidency.

Self-promotion is a signature characteristic of your personality. It bleeds out in every aspect of your speech and action. You never tire of highlighting your brand and promoting your products.

Since you continue to own and run, although surreptitiously through your sons, your family's business, it stands to reason that you would need to be pushing people to buy what you are selling. It, after all, puts money in your pocket and that is very important to you. And I'm sure you see it as being a shrewd businessman, taking advantage of every opportunity to increase your market share.

But you are the President of the United States, and this self-promotion of your brand comes across as crass and tactless. Not only that, you not only sell your wears, you also use taxpayer's dollars to line your pockets. I'm sure you will point out that you are donating your salary to charity and I think that is admirable since you don't "need" this money.

You are, though, constantly frequenting your own properties and utilizing your own facilities. But it is not just you. You have an entourage of hundreds who join you on these trips. Their bills are covered by the taxpayer as well. Of course, the news media probably uses your facilities, especially those relatively isolated, generating even more revenue for your brand.

All of this to say, your priority seems to make sure your brand is alive, well, and thriving. I don't know how well you are accomplishing this, but I know that it comes across as demeaning to the office you now hold.

THE BIBLE

People have always tried to misuse the Bible and justify their own actions based on a particular Scripture verse they have found which seems to support them and what they want to do. A member of your team was just the latest in a long line that has used the Bible to back up some particular perspective. Romans 13 leans itself to this since it clearly says that those who are followers of Christ are to be good citizens.

Of course, given that our country is built on the legacy of separation of Church and State, it seems to be quite ironic that a government official would be using the Bible to call on Americans to support their government. After all, not everyone in the United States is a Christian. Many do not even revere the Bible as a sacred text.

But the fact that a person honors the government under which they live does not mean that at some time, they might not run afoul of that same government. After all, Paul, author of the words found in Romans 13, found himself often in prison because of something he said or did with which a government official took umbrage.

Therefore, at the risk of offending you, Mr. President, I will refer you to another Scripture verse that I think you should take to heart. It is found in Luke 14:7-11

If you do not understand its significance, maybe the team member who read from Romans 13 will clarify it for you.

WINGING IT

t is incredible to think and see that this far into your presidency, you are still winging it. Going into meetings unprepared. Meeting with "foes" and "competitors," there are no "friends" alike on your own without an ounce of preparation. Oh, you claim that you have been preparing for this your whole life. I beg to differ.

That would be like me after I have run a million-dollar business telling you that I am capable of running a billion-dollar one. You would laugh me out of the room. Mr. President, you are running a trillion-dollar business by the seat of your pants.

Friends, foes, and competitors alike are shaking their collective heads and wondering what you will do next. Those you call competitors are taking advantage of you at every turn, and you are not even aware of it. Friends and those you call foes are trying to keep the ship of state together and not go under in the tsunami created by your ineptitude. The rest of us are holding on for dear life, afraid of what will come next.

You have the best, most skilled, and competent people in the world at your beck and call. Any one of a myriad of intelligent and capable diplomats and leaders would be glad for you to allow them to help you as you navigate these, for you, unchartered waters. But, no, you will not listen to them.

Instead, you listen to your favorite TV personality, who is as clueless as you are. You listen to those who curry to you and seek your favor. You listen to the crowd that eggs you on to brasher and more foolhardy decisions, which seem to be taking us down a road of no return.

Some day you will find out what the world already knows – you are not as good at "winging it" as you think you are. By then, of course, you will be out of office, and others will be trying to put back together a world you have ripped asunder. Others will be trying to rebuild bridges you have torn down. But unfortunately, most of us will be left to live with the legacy of destruction and desolation caused by your inept ability to govern because you thought you could wing it.

DISCOURAGED

My guess is that everyone on your staff is discouraged and getting more so by the day. The world around them is crumbling, and they can't do anything but continue to try and hold it together. Many of them see their future in jeopardy and, maybe, their very lives in peril.

They are tied to you and your frenzied way of governing. Their future is linked with yours, and the more they hear you speak, the more terrified they become because you seem to be going down a rabbit hole from which there is no return. Up is down, and in is out in this fantasy world you have created. Everything is topsy-turvy and spinning faster and faster out of control.

Those who came on board your bandwagon hoping to steer the ship of government toward a future of promise and hope are finding themselves in a hopeless estate. They can't but be disheartened and discouraged. What started out with so much promise is rapidly disintegrating into chaos.

You are going your merry way creating bedlam in your wake while the government tries to keep order. They are going one way while you are going 180 degrees in the opposite way. In the process, the country is being ripped asunder, everyone standing on the sidelines stultified, not knowing what to do to stem the pandemonium, which seems to be looming on the horizon.

Is it any wonder people have jumped ship? It is incredible that so many have continued to stick around. Apparently, they have nowhere else to go because they can't be naïve enough to think that they will be able to get you back on track and right this quickly sinking ship of state.

Of course, the human condition is one of eternal optimism. Those in your entourage are no different. They, I am sure, remain hopeful that the future will not be as bleak as it currently seems to be unfolding. They have confidence in their ability to make the bad go away and for the good to succeed. I hope they are right, but as of now, it looks like we are doomed.

Discouraged, that is the word. So much promise. So much hope. All gone in a flash. Discouraged.

DIRT

It would seem obvious that the Russian government in general and its President, in particular, have informed you that they have some "dirt" on you. This has come through loud and clear as the Russian President was asked that question directly, and he did not deny it. Then subsequently, in an interview, you indicated that you had spent a lot of time in Russia, and given the lifestyle you lived at the time and your prominence, there could be something.

Neither of these statements was an outright admission either on the part of the Russians or your own that salacious material exists. But all the indications are that there is something out there that you think might be embarrassing to you. And as a result, you are doing whatever you can to make sure it does not come out.

Mr. President, you have stated that you can stand in the middle of 5th Avenue in New York City and shoot someone, and no one would care. If that is true, and I believe you think it is, I do not understand why you allow yourself to be intimidated. Get the material out in the open. Tell the world what you did. Let everyone know what happened.

This way, the Russians would no longer have any leverage on you. It would be public knowledge, and your base will give you a pass. You might get some criticism from the liberal media, but you've faced that before and will again.

But maybe you don't think your people will give you a pass over this particular thing, and that is the reason you continue to duck and hide. You don't want to face the music out of fear that it will cost you your job. You are stuck and can't get out.

If that is true, then we are in real big trouble. The Russians will continue to pull your chain, and the United States will be in more peril than it has been in a very long time. They have never been timid about taking advantage of a foe whom they perceive as weak. And Mr. President, they see you as weak!

BLINDSIDED

Working for and with you, Mr. President, is a real rollercoaster ride. I am sure that your staff wonders what kind of ride they signed up for when they went to work for your administration. It can't be fun. It might have been at one time. The illusions of working in the White House. The idea of working for the President of the United States. The dream of making a difference. All of those were things surely were spinning through their heads as they said yes to your invitation to become part of your team. But now, I am sure most wonder if this can go on and how long they can hold on.

One of the most challenging parts of working for you is constantly being blindsided by your tweets. Not knowing what will happen each day until they look at your Twitter feed to see what you have most recently said. And then in a meeting or while being interviewed, hearing about some policy change or some decision, not from you, but out of the blue from their host. It can't be easy. Putting myself in their shoes, I can't imagine being constantly surprised by the mercurial leader for whom I work.

From what I have seen you have some remarkable people working on your staff. Some of these men and women are the best at what they do. And yet, you do not seem to listen to anything they say. You already have your mind made up, or you listen to some other voice because time and again you take your staff by surprise. This is obvious by the look on their face when confronted by some, often random person, who knows more than they do because they have seen your latest tweet.

I presume that you expect your staff to be supportive and loyal regardless of what haphazard direction your path takes. They are to maintain a stoic straight look on their face regardless of the surprising and often conflicting information coming from your feed. They are to back your play regardless of how reckless and dangerous they think it might be. After all, you are the President, and you are never wrong.

Working for you must be a thrill a minute, and I am sure that most wonder if they will ever wake up from the walking nightmare in which they currently find themselves. Most hope, I am sure but are not convinced that tomorrow will be any better. They continue to hold on, hoping that they can make it to the end of the ride. But their confidence is gone. Their excitement has dissipated. They are just going through the motions hoping against hope that the future will not judge them too harshly. Of course, if the past is any forecast of the future, they will probably not be around you long enough to see that future.

TREASON

The Merriam-Webster dictionary defines treason as *1: the offense of attempting by overt acts to overthrow the government of the state to which the offender owes allegiance or to kill or personally injure the sovereign or the sovereign's family;* or *2: the betrayal of a trust.*

Generally, we think of this as an agent of another government who has worked to bring down the country to which he or she should be loyal, given their citizenship or work. Sometimes this word is bandied around recklessly as a pejorative, as an attempt to intimidate or frighten someone. Soon after assuming the presidency, some who opposed you even began using this term to describe your actions and decisions. I am sure they want to point out how you had crossed a line according to them.

But you seemingly shrugged it off and kept on going. Lately, though, the word has been used to characterize some of the things which have happened around you. And some of those using this term, in the past, have been allies and even supporters of yours. They don't indicate that you are guilty of treason but that some action taken could be construed as treasonous.

Again, it seems like water off a duck's back. What they say not only does not seem to affect you, but you continue to do what they abhor. And in some cases, you double down and increase what you had been doing. I think I finally understand why this is true.

It is your understanding that, as President, you cannot commit treason against the United States. As President, you embody the United States of America. You are the United States, and, therefore, you can't commit treason against yourself. Since you and the United States are one and the same, everything you do is in the country's best interest.

Anyone who knows or has seen you understands how much you value yourself. Time and time again, you have made it clear that you are the most brilliant and important person in the world. And it is impossible not to be aware of how much worth you place on yourself. Therefore, how can anyone ever think that you would do something that would damage your person and, by extension, the United States whom you embody?

There is no treason because you cannot commit treason against yourself. What more needs to be said?

NO COLLUSION

Mr. President, you never seem to tire of railing against the injustices you think have been perpetrated against you by the previous administration and various governmental agencies. It is a never-ending part of your Twitter feed. Unfortunately, you keep repeating the same old refuse you always dish out. There is nothing new in spite of being currently in charge of all of the avenues of information, which would provide further insight into what really happened.

You don't bring new material to the game. You don't seem to avail yourself of the myriad of resources at your disposal to ascertain what really happened. You just trash the very agencies who might be able to help you and the American public finally gain some clarity about all the things you find odious about the previous administration and the various arms of government. It would seem that you are more interested in carping about the wrongs that were supposedly done against you than helping us find out what really happened.

What's more, you seem content with lambasting those who are trying to discover the truth. Your crosshairs are centered on those who are arduously working to determine what crimes might have taken place. This is the very task that would give credence to your diatribe, and yet you cannot let them do their job without ridiculing and deriding them.

What gives? Are you more interested in hearing yourself talk? Is the sound of your voice so much more important than making sure the guilty are discovered and correcting those things which gave opportunity to the miscreants who sought to harm you?

If you are really seriously upset about what you claim so loudly happened to you, then stop chiding, scolding, rebuking, and admonishing these men and women who are tirelessly working to discover the truth. Get off your bandwagon and start making a difference. After all, you are in a unique position to accomplish something and not just complain about it. Mr. President, be the agent of change, don't just rail.

INFORMATION

A reoccurring thought keeps coming to mind as I read your Twitter feed, Mr. President. Is the information you are getting from your intelligence and law enforcement agencies helping you? The reason for the question is not just the fact that you seem to question what they say, but nothing has changed from your rhetoric since you were a candidate.

It would stand to reason that as President, you would have access to much more information than you were ever privy to as a candidate for office. In effect, every office and agency in the government is at your beck and call. You can elicit information about any subject from any of them and demand that they tell you the facts and give you all the background information.

Having access to all this information, though, has not changed your talking points. Therefore, one of two things seems to be taking place. One, all this new information is clarifying and affirming your positions. If that is the case, we would ask you to present this information. Don't just continue to shadow box; give us the details so that we can understand what has gotten you so upset and what keeps you so distraught.

The other possibility is that you continue to eschew the information from the agencies you now control. You famously did this before the election claiming the information you already had was far superior to any that you were being given in the briefings offered to you as a candidate. We understood that this could very well be true since the government is guarded about what it shares, and with your resources, you might have been able to gather substantially better information from much more willing sources.

But you are now the President, and it stands to reason that those agencies which at one time kept you in the dark, as a candidate, would now be totally forthcoming since, after all, you are the boss. Therefore, should this be the case, the only conclusion from this argument is that the information you are now receiving conflicts with your cherished beliefs and opinions. Leading us to understand that you would rather hold on to these ideas than admit that you are wrong.

This obvious conclusion creates significant problems because if you are holding onto these petty issues and unwilling to allow this new information to inform your actions, what other data have you been given which also is not being acted upon. Are you making decisions without the latest and most important information simply because you do not want to be confused with the facts? Are you creating hostile situations with friends and foes alike due to some preconceived notion you have been carrying around, without any justification or substantiation by the facts you now have at hand?

Mr. President, this is dangerous to us as a people and to the world. Either give us the facts which back up your diatribes or begin listening to your intelligence agencies so that you can act on the best

information and not just some preconceived ideas you may have been
harboring due to personal issues you have encountered in the past.

207

SHOUTING

One can only presume that hollering and shouting have gotten you what you wanted along the way. In my book, they are similar, if not the same, as bullying. Again, this is the kind of conduct that evidently has produced results for you, and those results have been gratifying.

Being the loudest voice in the room or on the internet may make you feel good, but seldom does it produce good viable results. It may intimidate those who are easily frightened, but those results are only momentary and very fleeting. It may feel good at the moment, but often those feelings are short-lived.

Unfortunately, and you should understand this very well, the pushback is overwhelming and often unwarrantedly harsh. It is seldom a tit for tat. It is ramped up and often punitive.

Intimidation is the name of the game. Much like bullying, hollering's objective is to get the object of ridicule to back down and cower. The more fear that can be imposed, the more likely you are to get your way.

The problem is some of those who have been the subject of your ire and abuse have nothing to lose. Not only are they beyond the reach of your maneuvers they also have become past masters at using terror tactics of their own. Like you, they too use these methods to gain dominance over their adversaries, and like you, they have been successful in the past.

Albert Einstein is famously quoted as giving the following definition of insanity. "Doing the same thing over and over again and expecting a different result." I am not suggesting that you are insane, but I am suggesting that it might be wise for you to begin using some other strategy to get what you want. I think you have played out this hand, and it will not continue working. Try something different or continue to get the poor results you have been getting. That is not good for you or for the country.

WISHFUL THINKING

Repeating something over and over again, hoping that it will be true, and trying to use that method as a ploy to convince others seems to be in vogue at this time. From my perspective, this is wishful thinking.

Just because you say something is one way doesn't mean it is. Saying that you didn't say what you said and having others vouch for you does not obviate what everyone heard. It is too late; the cat is out of the bag. Regardless of how much you would like for it not to be, it is.

Now, even some of those who work for you or have worked for you in the past, Mr. President, are using this same strategy. I guess they think that if you think you can get away with it, they should be able to do so as well. Unfortunately, life doesn't work that way.

We are held accountable for the words we speak. No one should be more aware of this than you, Mr. President. After all, you castigated your opponents unmercifully during the campaign when something came out in a way they had not intended. You did not let up but kept after them day after day. Is it any wonder that the press uses this same tactic when it comes to your words? Why are you so surprised and feel abused?

This is how the game is played, and thinking that anyone is going to give you or anyone in your administration a pass is wishful thinking. It isn't going to happen. Not only will every word you utter, in whatever format it appears, be scrutinized, but those who oppose you will throw them back in your face much like you did to your opposition.

You seem to think now that you are President, you should be exempt from this kind of analysis. Although you were unrelenting when it came to your predecessor, you seem to think that people are treating you unfairly as they grill your staff over the nuances of your utterances.

Get prepared, Mr. President; it is only going to get worse. And it will continue to get hotter. As they say, "If you can't stand the heat, get out of the kitchen." You chose this path; now you have to live with it.

PETTY

M r. President, it is quite petty of you to threaten those who disagree with you with revoking their clearances. But petty seems to be your middle name. There are probably other more colorful words that would and should characterize you and how you treat those who speak out against you or say things with which you disagree. But I've chosen the word petty because that sums up the kinds of dribble which I have heard coming out of the White House as it tries to justify abusing those whom you evidently find offensive.

The word means "of little importance'. Synonyms include "trivial," "trifling," "minor," "small," "unimportant," "insignificant," "inconsequential," "inconsiderable," "negligible," "paltry," "puny," "footling," "pettifogging," and "piddling."

The very fact that you, Mr. President, have threatened those who speak out against you with retaliation and punishment demonstrates the puny person you really are. It takes a trifling person to take trivial matters of inconsequential value and blow them out of proportion. Anyone who does this can only be described as small, unimportant, and insignificant.

Telling your press secretary to lash out at these men and women who have served the country and using this tactic to try to coerce and intimidate them is beneath the office of the President. This makes you appear a piddling fool since everyone in this country has the right to express themselves without fear of reprisals. After all, we don't, yet, live in a police state where government officials can do whatever they like, and the rest of us have to grin and bear it.

You, Mr. President, have the right to say whatever you like as long as it is not damaging to others and the country. This, though, goes to the very core of what this country stands for, and the American public cannot and should not take this kind of threat lightly.

Fortunately for you, and unfortunately for the country, the 24-hour news cycle will mean that tomorrow people will have forgotten about it. That is until you bring it back up, making further outrageous threats and continuing to try to defame and frighten those who in any way speak out against you. Since this is your MO, someday someone will hold you accountable.

FACT CHECK

In this day and age, when it is so easy to confirm information, which is in the public domain, it is a wonder you, Mr. President, continue day after day spouting facts that can easily be determined to be blatantly false. Don't you have a team who can help you know what is "out there" so that you will not continue to share things that are not accurate? Or is it that you don't care, you will say what you want regardless of whether it is true or not? I hope it is the former.

If your staff is failing you, fire them. You have made your mark on social media by the two words; you're fired! Use them to eliminate the dead weight that keeps you in the dark and not protect you from saying inaccurate things. You need to use them. They need to have your back. They need to help you. They need to make sure your "facts" line up with those in the public domain. Otherwise, you will be accused of being FAKE NEWS, and people will stop believing you.

Even your base, those who have stood by you through thick and thin, will begin to doubt your word and question what you are saying if you continue to say easily verifiable things. They, too, can look up on Google and see if something happened how you claim it did. They, too, can search the web for information that will substantiate or refute what you claim to be true. I would like to think that they are not ignorant, gullible people. They want the best for the country, and they hold you in high esteem. But if you keep telling them things that are not accurate, they will begin to lose confidence in you, regardless of how loyal they are.

They want a President they can trust, and one who continually lies to them does not demonstrate himself to be very trustworthy. From all reports, your supporters already mistrust those in office. They feel that they have been lied to and have been misused. If you continue to spread falsehood, they will begin believing that they have been caught up in a massive game of bait and switch.

On the campaign, you claimed you would shoot straight with your supporters. Over and over again, you said that you were the outsider who would clean things up in Washington and change the way things are done. Yet we often see someone who uses the same old smoke and mirrors to try to pull the wool over our eyes, thinking they can hoodwink us, and we will not know any better.

That is not fair to the country and certainly not fair to your loyal fan base. They deserve better. Check your facts and give us what you claimed you would. Tell us the unvarnished truth and not the lies we have been so accustomed to getting from inside the Beltway. Be honest with us and not the deceitful, corrupt politician we have unfortunately grown accustomed to seeing in public office.

FIXATION

Becoming fixed on something is often problematic in this variable and changing world. If you can only focus on one thing or aspect, you often miss the subtleties of life around you, which give you options you otherwise would never have seen. Of course, there are times when concentrating all your energies on one thing is what the issue requires. Like, for instance, focusing on your wife to the exclusion of all the other women who surround you. But I'm sure you realized, Mr. President, there is a difference between focus and fixation.

Fixating evidently comes easy to you instead of focusing, which seems to be something you find difficult. An adage says if the only thing you have is a hammer, everything looks like a nail. Fixating falls into that category. Whereas focusing allows you to see all aspects of the issue, fixating causing you to be very one-dimensional.

Fixating doesn't allow you to move past the object of your fixation. In fact, you become so consumed by that fixation that you lose all reason when it comes to that subject. Often this cripples you emotionally and tarnishes your relationships, especially should anyone try to help you. The very people who are trying to help you move on and gain perspective often become the focus of your ire because they are not as consumed by the fixation as you are.

One of the problems with fixations is that they cloud your mind and do not allow you to think clearly. You are so consumed by the fixation that all else becomes trite and pedestrian. Nothing is as important as fixing your fixation. Everyone needs to know about it, and every ounce of everyone's energies needs to be as consumed as you with making sure that this fixation is taking care of and done so quickly. Not only that, but everything becomes twisted, and as with the hammer, everything becomes a nail or, in your case, the object of your fixation or, maybe more accurately, your obsession.

Most people become overwhelmed with just one fixation, but you, Mr. President, have several which absorb much of your time. It is a wonder you have time to do anything else because of these issues. And unfortunately, the twisted thinking brought about by your fixations has caused you to see things that are not there and declare as verified, things that simply cannot be.

One example serves to prove my point. The President of Russia has publicly admitted that he wanted you in the White House and is pleased that you are President. One of your fixations, among others, is the "fact," according to you, that you and you alone won the race for President. No one played a part in helping you accomplish this feat. Therefore, Russia could not have worked on your behalf because you did not need any help.

What's more, they would not help you in the future because you have been so "hard" on them due to all the sanctions and other things you have done to them since taking office. Of course, your predecessor or Congress did the vast majority of the things for which you take credit. But that is another issue.

The Democratic Party, on the other hand, cannot win the White House without significant support from others. Therefore, you claim that Russia is backing the Democratic Party against you. This is despite the President of Russia's support of you. This twisted logic on your part allows you to salve two of your fixations – winning on your own and attacking the Democratic Party. Regardless of how absurd it seems to anyone else, it makes sense to you and, therefore, must be true.

COUNTERPUNCH

One of the characteristics of your personality, of which you seem very proud, is your ability to counterpunch. You mentioned this during the campaign and continue to do it voraciously. Often it would seem you are really shadow boxing since there is no one on the other side; your opponent has long since left the ring.

The irony of these punches and counterpunches, most of which seem to come from you on both sides, is they continue to highlight things anyone else would have long ago allowed to die in ignominy.

Every week, and sometimes daily, you mention your opponent from the previous election. Most of your predecessors quickly moved past the election, and their opponents have been lost to history. In fact, most people would be hard-pressed to name even the most recent loser in the quadrennial event. On the other hand, yours continues to be in the news and making headlines. Most of those headlines are thanks to your naming her constantly in your Twitter feed.

The investigation which has caught so much of your ire also is something most people would have allowed to play out in obscurity. On the other hand, you have to mention it daily, if not several times a day. Investigations routinely take place in various venues around the country all the time. Most are never noted by the news media and certainly do not garner headlines. Obviously, since this one is about you, Mr. President, it would gather more scrutiny. But, except for your need to mention it constantly, it probably would chart its ordinary course with little fanfare until such time as there was an indictment or trial. This one, on the other hand, makes headlines on rumors, suspicion, and innuendo, all of which at other times would have been ignored. But you can't ignore anything. You have to counterpunch even if there is nothing worth punching in the first place.

This is also the case with the opposition party. As you so often point out, the economy continues to roar. Seemingly with no end in sight. The unemployment rate continues at historic lows while inflation is barely visible by past standards given this kind of economy. If it weren't for you creating problems with our trading partners, everyone would be happy, and the stock market, although at historic highs, would be in the stratosphere. Given all this excellent news, the bi-elections should be a no-brainer. Your party should be at the forefront of every poll. And yet, it is struggling, even against a disorganized and radicalized opposition who does not seem to know where they are going. Part, maybe most, of the reason is you, Mr. President.

Your absurd statements about the Democratic Party being helped by the Russians. You're clamoring for servers, although the information from these devices has already been distributed to the officials who need them. You're chiming in on every minor insignificant opposition politician, bullying and calling them names. All these tactics draw attention (and money) to a party that is struggling to know who it is and where it is going.

This makes me wonder if you really are doing yourself, your party, or the country any service by continuing these antics. Each counterpunch gains national notoriety and yet achieves nothing. Each verbal slash draws attention to things and people who otherwise would be forgotten. Each confrontation leaves you weaker and others stronger. Are you trying to undermine your future and your legacy? Is this the reason for all of this? I doubt it, given your personality traits, but what you are doing is not accomplishing what I think you would like for it to do. I'm sure people in your entourage have told you this. Listen to them and get on with the business of making this country great.

RETRIBUTION

Mr. President you seem to have a penchant for wanting to get even. You want to get back at those you think have wronged you, and you will do whatever it takes to make sure they get what you think they deserve. Often this means doing things that seem petty, mean, cruel, and downright ugly. But you don't care, they deserve retribution, and you are going to give it to them.

Fortunately, you pale compared to some of your predecessors who have taken the country to war over seemingly inconsequential events or mistakes. I'm reminded of an incident on one of our warships when a young sailor accidentally dropped a grenade in the magazine, sinking the ship. One of your predecessors used this as an excuse to declare war and eventually strip Spain of most of its colonies. Or when a supposed incident in the Gulf of Tonkin drew the United States into a long, protracted, and often reviled war. Or when a reported stockpile of weapons of mass destruction gave one of your predecessors an excuse to depose a dictator who had been a thorn in his and his father's side.

But, never the less, your acts of retribution take their toll. They cast doubt on the rule of law. They seem to embolden your followers and staff to do things they might otherwise not ever consider. Like when a supporter inspired by your rhetoric took an unprovoked slug at a man being taken away in handcuffs. Or when ICE agents abuse their power and violate the spirit of the law, if not its very letter.

Unfortunately, your example seems to be drawing us down a rabbit hole, creating a most discordant culture and society. One where differing opinions are not acceptable. An America where it is no longer acceptable for people to hold conflicting ideas, views, or opinions. One in which the very foundation of free speech guaranteed by the First Amendment of the Constitution seems to be imperiled. A place where we are not interested in what people think; we just want to know if they agree with us—a divided and polemical environment that leads to discord and fighting.

Maybe it is time to "turn the other cheek," to allow others to voice their opinions and ask their questions without fear of retribution. Perhaps it is time for us to be the kinder, gentler America which in the past came to the aid of the world, fought other's battles, and was looked upon for help and support.

HERO

Mr. President, you have the drive to be the hero of your own reality show. You need to be able to ride in on your white horse and save the day. Or better yet, fly in on your jet plane draped in Old Glory, taking on all comers, and emerge victorious, having vanquished all foes. Of course, for this latter to happen, you will need to repaint the aircraft, which for some reason can't be done until your term is over.

Life is a reality show, and if the right scenarios do not naturally present themselves, you need to orchestrate events to make them run according to the script you have developed in your mind. The script has you as the central figure who is there to save the damsel or country in distress. Of course, this often means creating a problem from which you will save those imperiled regardless of how artificial it seems to all those looking on. This is your show, and you will do with it whatever you want.

Once again, you walk out of a meeting with a person, only days after you had highlighted how horrible a foe they were, who needs to be, at least tamed, if not totally vanquished. You walk to the podium and tell the American people that now that you have met the enemy, they are no longer to be feared. They are now as docile as a new puppy. You have tamed the ferocious opponent, and they have cowered to you. In the past, they had overwhelmed everyone else, but you have fearlessly taken them on, and they have submitted to your will.

They have played their part perfectly in your scripted reality show. Once again, you are the hero, and everyone is in awe of your prowess and skill. Whereas others have tried and failed, you have succeeded. You can do what no one in history has ever been able to accomplish.

The hero stands. The crowd stares in awe and wonder. The enemy is humbled and shamed. All is well with the world until the next foe needs to be conquered. And once again, the American public will be able to depend on their All-American Hero to come to the rescue draped in Old Glory and vanquishing all foes.

RACISM

Mr. President, you have vociferously denied being a racist. Your denials have come repeatedly and from many of your surrogates. You have even highlighted your friendships with those of color on several occasions. But as with many other things, these denials seem hollow and maybe even a little trite.

Frankly, your defense of your character regarding racism is, in reality, laughable. Although you have highlighted people of color with whom you have had dealings and refer to them as "friends," this is really disingenuous. As pointed out elsewhere, you really do not have friends. You have people whom you use and discard, but even those closest to you would find it difficult to fit into the "friend" mold. This is all the more so with those of color, whom you really use to promote yourself rather than genuinely drawing close to them on a personal basis required by the word friend.

And whereas you have been accused of using a racial slur which has been used to call into question the humanity of a race of people, you find it easy to call into question the humanity of an individual by calling her a "dog." I find them equally offensive, as I think most people do.

Of course, this is not the only incident where you vilify those you find objectionable by slurring their character and calling into question their very humanity. Therefore, your mere defense gives substance to your accuser and, once again, highlights your lack of sound judgment.

If, in fact, you are not a racist, then your words and actions need to reflect that reality. Neither of these shows the kind of regard for your fellow human being, which would characterize someone you purport to be. The people with whom you surround yourself, the words you use to demean those you find objectionable, and how you use people for your personal advantage all give lie to your defense and make it ever more obvious that your accusers are correct.

It would seem to me that the "real you" is coming out from behind the persona you created to befuddle the masses, confuse your opponents, and enamor your supporters. Unfortunately for you, the masses are becoming aware of your ploys, your opponents understand who you are, and even your loyal supporters are gradually growing weary of your antics. It may not be enough to cause your immediate demise, but surely history will be a harsher judge than those who are currently propping you up, often to fulfill their own agendas.

DITTO

As I finish this series of "Op-ed" pieces, I realize that often I could have said "ditto." Mr. President, it would seem that you never tire of saying the same old things over and over again. Blaming the same people for issues and never taking responsibility for your own failings.

At some point, it becomes repetitive ad nauseam. You may never tire of repeating yourself, but I am afraid that my audience would grow very tired of hearing me counter your tweets over and over again with the same kinds of bewilderment and disbelief. I have tried not to repeat myself, but it becomes increasingly more difficult as we go over the same material and plow the same ground time and time again.

If I was giving you counsel, I would say, "grow up and move on." Of course, I am not sure that you accept counsel from anyone, much less someone who is totally unknown, like me. It would seem even those in your inner circle have given up on trying to help you out. They just allow you to go on and on without any guidelines from the sidelines. I am sure they have tried but have realized that it is totally futile and useless.

Therefore, I will not attempt what others have tried. What's more, I will not even continue to try to shine a light on the absurdities of what you say. Time will tell if others begin to wake up and see you for what you really are. Or if you are correct, people don't care as long as you give them a good show.

CONCLUSION

Maybe King Solomon's words are warning enough:

> A worthless person, a wicked man,
> goes about with crooked speech,
> winks with his eyes, signals with his feet,
> points with his finger,
> with perverted heart devises evil,
> continually sowing discord;
> therefore, calamity will come upon him suddenly;
> in a moment, he will be broken beyond healing.
> There are six things that the LORD hates,
> seven that are an abomination to him:
> haughty eyes, a lying tongue,
> and hands that shed innocent blood,
> a heart that devises wicked plans,
> feet that make haste to run to evil,
> a false witness who breathes out lies,
> and one who sows discord among brothers.

Proverbs 6:12–19 (English Standard Version)

ACKNOWLEDGEMENTS

A book is never written in a void. Events and people surround the author, each of which influences what is written. This, of course, is never more apparent than in this work. Everyday events and tweets have served as the background for most, if not all, of the chapters.

People have also played a significant role. This book would have remained the musings of a frustrated author if it weren't for several people who have encouraged me along the way. I will not mention their names for many reasons. I might leave someone out who deserves to be mentioned, and I would not want to do that. Another reason is that, although they have encouraged me, the words are my own, and I would not want them to suffer the consequences of supporting me in this endeavor.

You might question this last statement, but we live in a world in which it is difficult and sometimes dangerous to express an opinion. It would seem that a growing number of people are not interested in hearing other people's views. They only want to know if you agree with their opinion. If not, you will suffer the bullying that has become all too common.

Therefore, I mention just a few people, with fear and trepidation, who have made it possible for this book to be published. Brant Elmore, Pete Flannery, and Joan West graciously read through the manuscript and offered valuable insight to make it better and communicate more effectively. And my daughter, Rebekah Law, pulled together the elements to make the cover appealing and striking. Thank you each for the part you played in helping me along the way.

My family, especially my wife, has been longsuffering as they have listened to my comments and, at times, argued with my conclusions. I appreciate their patience and love more than I can ever say.

ABOUT THE AUTHOR

Although I am not currently a registered Republican, I adhere to many, if not most, of the values that have been foundational to this political party. That said, I feel marginalized by the rhetoric coming from the White House and those on the far right. They have moved so far that they have left me in their dust.

I have lived under three of the longest-tenured dictators of the 20th Century. I have found that dictatorial governments on the right and the left are not far from each other. In fact, I would say that in most ways, they are identical. Their main aim is to protect the power elite, particularly the dictator. Their tactics and methods are similar, if not identical. Fear is their greatest weapon. Unfortunately, I find those same characteristics rampant in today's White House.

Being an evangelical Christian, I value life, including those yet to be born. That means, though, that I value all life. The way policies have been implemented would seem to reflect a valuation or gradation of life – some are more valuable than others. The constant push and fervor for the unborn does not give way to policies protecting those already born and in need. What of the ill, those with mental issues, those in need of education, etc.? It would seem that those issues have all been given to the Democrats while the Republicans only care about one issue – abortion.

Living within your means is a personal value I hold very dear; I wish that our government did as well. I am afraid that we are mortgaging our children's future as we fund boondoggles, and politicians line their supporters' pockets in an attempt to stay in office. I find it interesting that the only balanced budget in recent memory came during a Democrats' administration.

Constitutional law is a doctrine that has kept our country on an even keel through many trials. I have difficulty with those judges who find it necessary to "legislate from the bench." This is not their role, and they should refrain from doing it. The problem is that they often feel obligated to act because Congress is not doing its job, and the office of the President is not giving the leadership necessary to move Congress to act.

Congress and the President must begin to deliver well-thought-out legislation that solves problems, not coddle their supporters. The issues, immigration, deficit spending, public education, trade, security, guns, etc., are not going away, and until legislation is passed to deal with them, they will only worsen.

Finally, the older I get, the more I realize that as categorical as I would like to be with the above-named issues and others, more heart, and compassion are also needed. We are a people of love and care. That needs to be part of everything we do, or we will lose what makes us the great nation we have been.

The author can be contacted at: mr.presidentsaywhat@gmail.com

Author's Note: Reviews are gold for authors. Please consider writing a book review on www.Amazon.com if you liked the book.